Canticle of Returning

Canticle of Returning

by
William J. Brown

 ENROUTE

ENROUTE

En Route Books & Media
5705 Rhodes Avenue, St. Louis, MO 63109
Contact us at contactus@enroutebooksandmedia.com

E-book ISBN: 978-0-9996670-2-6

Paperback ISBN: 978-1-950108-63-3

LCCN: 9780999470497

Te Deum

To God and to the Lamb, Who is the great "I AM,"*

Heaven and Earth are full of your glory

Ad Deum

* Hymn, "What Wondrous Love is This," text by Alexander Means (1801–1883), verse 2, line 3, in *Worship*, Fourth Ed. (Chicago: GIA Publications, Inc., 2011), #641.

Table of Contents

Preface

These twenty-five brief essays consider how you might invest your time on earth in ways that will bridge a path to eternal life. Although I'm Catholic, you need not be to benefit from this. And I won't try to convert you or tout Catholicism. While I naturally consider my Catholic faith to be "the one true religion," everyone else thinks the same way about *their* personal beliefs! Regardless of your religion, my aim is to bolster your belief system by beefing-up your awareness of and commitment to God. *Your* God. And if you're unsure about your religious affiliation or uncertain about being affiliated with any religion at all, this book will help strengthen your spirituality. That's something you definitely ought to embrace with a passion, as it's a readily available way of getting far more out of life.

We reap what we sow and only have limited planting seasons to avail of. I wasted some of mine during a period of drifting away—ceasing to be mindful of God—and while afflicted with critical illnesses. But challenges can actually prompt us to develop a closer relationship with God, experience spiritual growth, increase religiosity, and even improve our day-to-day lives. That was my experience, as it can also be yours. Fortunately, *you* don't have to get cancer or forget about God! Just read these essays, share my experiences, and observe how your very *being* changes, gradually, for the better: be confidently patient.

Magister, the Latin word for "teacher," makes my life's work sound more laudable than it does in English. I first aspired late in life to serve as a magister on behalf of God by becoming a deacon. Unfortunately, I was already too old to undertake the five years' preparatory study to qualify; the Catholic Church doesn't want to invest in someone unlikely to serve for a meaningful time after being ordained. (At seventy-eight years of age, with cancer, I was bucking the odds.) I hope someone else hears the call I can't answer, and what a happy coincidence it would be if they turned out to be one of you readers!

That said, the principal objective of this book is not to inspire vocations to holy orders. My goal is simply to bring you much closer to God, albeit by way of an unusual initial methodology: by recounting how I came to be a "fallen-away Catholic." Experience is a great teacher, but she always gives the test before we learn her lesson! After reading about my "away" route, I trust that you'll be both savvy and wary enough to avoid it.

I was "away" for decades, yet only late in that period did the feeling of being a sinner finally set in. I'll share those times—which contrast with more recent days of my life—and teach you from my mis-steps. While the source of these lessons may be negative, their message is reassuringly positive. Of course, you'll probably suffer some setbacks (I can't prevent their occurrence), but if my efforts here succeed, you should have a much easier time of it.

I learned a lot from my "fall," but by far the most valuable aftermath of this entire experience is how much more prayerful and closer to God my life has become. The "Remaining" and "Sustaining" portions of this book comprise roughly half of its entire length so you can draw closer to God by becoming more prayerful—and not fall in the first place! That's my motivation for writing: to prevent others from falling, and facilitate recoveries by those who do.

In my experience, as one grows evermore near to God, the better life becomes. It really doesn't matter where you start, but drifting *away* from God is hardly a prerequisite to experiencing the gladness that awaits those who steer a course *toward* God. As for *when* you start, sooner is better than later. What if *you* want to become a deacon?

These writings are intended to be of benefit regardless of how you perceive God. And even if you do not at all, I hope the thoughts expressed here will resonate with you. All too many Catholics and other Christians today have grown lax in their religious practices—which means they're missing out on the fullness this life offers when lived in loving pursuit of God. I hope this book serves to help many rediscover (or perhaps find for the first time) that joy. Just stick with me, while appreciating that this is a *gradual* process.

Life is too short not to *love God* for most if not all the time we have. Do so, and your stay on earth is likely to prove more purposeful, meaningful, and even enjoyable. I want to encourage the development of lives founded on love, fortified by faith, and fostered by prayer…and *I want you to experience that life!*

Since I'm neither a theologian nor a saint, nothing here should intimidate you or prove particularly confounding. I'm going to guide you by reference to some way-points from my own journey. Not that you'll want to trace my steps, given that there's a far better course to follow—charted for us two thousand years ago by Jesus Christ. And *your* pursuit of that path will likely prove far less daunting than you might think.

"Come to me," Jesus said, "and I will give you rest. Take my yoke upon you and . . . find rest for yourselves. For my yoke is easy, and my burden light." As recounted in Matthew11:28–30 (USCCB), Christ's promise may seem hard to believe, but it comes true because when we labor under the weight of sin, our burden *is* great, yet once freed from sin, God's yoke becomes considerably easier to bear. Rejecting temptation is not easy, but prayerful inclusion of God in our daily lives is the secret weapon. By spurning evil and being loyal to God, we stand not only to find that *rest* that Jesus promises but also to derive great *joy* from taking up with God![1]

---

1   I can promise—based on my personal experience—that by becoming more prayerful, drawing more close to and trusting in a loving God, you *will* have greater joy in your life. I'm far from alone. Several recent studies substantiate that. *See* David Briggs, "How perceptions of God help determine self-esteem, mental health," *Ahead of the Trend*, September 25, 2017, Association of Religion Data Archives (The ARDA). <blogs.thearda.com/trend/featured/how-perceptions-of-god-help-determine-self-esteem-mental-health/>. ("[I]ndividuals who believe in a loving God who takes a personal interest in them appear more likely to reap a host of mental health benefits…[ranging] from being less likely to be anxious or depressed to having a greater sense of optimism and hope even while facing stressful situations. And the benefits accrue to people of all ages.")

Introduction

I was raised Catholic (some would call me a "cradle Catholic") by a genuinely saintly mother. Beneficiary of Catholic education all the way—even through law school. The odds of my gliding through life without any major, long-term deviations from God's Will were highly favorable. So, what happened? Chalk it up to our secularized society in which the role of religion has become sorely diminished. If someone like me is susceptible to *falling away*, then pretty near everyone is; since it could even happen to you, preventive measures are called for.

Let's begin by considering what occurs when one falls away: what are the hallmarks of "leaving"? Having fallen (though since recovered), I can report that it's not very likely you would even notice a fall from grace was ever happening. I never did, and therefore made no effort to keep it from progressing. There is no *fall*, really, more like an imperceptibly slow *slide*. The process can be seen as devilishly deceitful when considered in hindsight: it sets off no attention-grabbing alarms as your soul grows increasingly somnolent. Eventually, after becoming *aware*—should you be so fortunate as to gain that realization—it's quite difficult to get back.

While my soul slept, God stopped being a part of my life: no prayers, no Sunday Mass . . . . While always believing in God, I somehow lost my Catholic faith and stopped practicing my religion. At no point during my "away" years did I suspect there was no God. The problem was that God did not occur to me at all—never crossed my mind. My entire being gradually became absorbed with *this world* and *this life*: the temporal. This gradual transition was well beyond my conscious awareness. I am quite certain, however, that *God was aware* of my departure and prolonged absence.

> While "fallen away," I never doubted God's existence:
> worse, God never crossed my mind.

Perhaps you think there's no way that even a "superior being" could keep track of the 7.5 billion human beings currently on earth (including insignificant me). Guess again! Fifty years ago, the United States first landed a manned module on the moon.

Today, your *car* harbors greater computing power than guided our Apollo astronauts to their destination! As the speed and capacity of cutting-edge computers advance, we should find ever more plausible the notion of a God capable of keeping tabs on everyone—and naturally disposed to do so.

✦

Ironically, as science has advanced, belief in God has declined. That statistic ought to be trending in the opposite direction. But then again, the Catholic Church did not always deal well with scientific breakthroughs—as when Copernicus and Galileo espoused heliocentricity and Charles Darwin theorized about evolution—yet what was challenging for a while certainly shouldn't be any longer. God's role as creator is neither diminished nor disproved by a creature like the coelacanth; there never was any conflict or contradiction between origin of the species, or evolution, and existence of God as the "uncaused cause" of our universe.

We continue to unearth scientific discoveries every day, solving riddles to which the answers were always there, waiting to be uncovered. It's generally observable that the *complexity* of each of these new discoveries is greater than those made in the past. Bear in mind that St. Thomas Aquinas, the great theologian, proffered complexity and order (or design) in the universe among his proofs—grounds for believing in God!

What if scientific advancements eventually included an ability to synthesize life forms from exclusively inanimate components? Were this to occur tomorrow, my faith in the existence of God would hardly be shaken. Even so, my religious beliefs are far from "blind faith." Beyond being attributable to parental influence (not by indoctrination, but rather from their good example), my beliefs are soundly supported by personal inclination—which is to say human reason.

The gravitational forces on earth and the rest of our universe (whose vastness we have yet fully to comprehend), our sun-centric solar system's evolving life forms, their RNA/DNA building blocks, quantum mechanics, and all the rest—seem to suggest a higher power, rather than evidencing there to be no God. More simply put: science is not at war with belief in God.

✦

When I ultimately awakened to the fact of my "fall," Easter was approaching—the most solemn time during the liturgical year. But why did that matter to me, after having been away for so many years? Because I remained, at least nominally, "Catholic." My religion had not changed—either to "none" or to one different from the original. This integral part of my identity ever since childhood never died completely, despite that for the longest time there were absolutely no signs of life. Fortunately, the Good Shepherd never forgets about the lamb that's gone missing.

Upon first opening my eyes, what I saw came as a shock: *massa pescati*, a sinful mess. I wondered how I got so lost as to end up wandering about aimlessly in an evermore secularized world. A nagging feeling began to develop, that this recent period of my life was marked by inattention to the direction in which I headed or the destination sought, and it ultimately became dissatisfying, even disappointing. Some higher purpose was clearly being called for.

Hurry after Christ to catch elegant solutions for challenges we face— This life's travails on the course we run—in our human race.

"Maybe I should turn around and go back up that path . . . rediscover God, learn from Christ's Resurrection," I thought. And thus began my long, slow, all-too-hesitant trek of "returning." I continue on, eager to see where this leads. The scenery is getting better by the day. Will you join me?

✦

Try to be again like the wide-eyed child that you once were by allowing yourself to experience wonderment with daily observations. Look up at each morning's sky:

Praise with elation,
Praise every morning,
God's re-creation
Of the new day!"²

---

2   Hymn, "Morning has Broken," text by Eleanor Farjeon, verse 3, from *The Children's Bells*, in *Worship*, #847. *See also* text of the hymn "Lord of All Helpfulness," by Jan Struther (1901–1953), © Oxford University Press: "Your bliss in our hearts, Lord, at the break of the day," in *Worship*, #686, with subsequent verses calling for strength at noon, love at the eve of the day, and peace at day's end.

Gaze at the stars shining through a dark night. Let your everyday discoveries and experiences of living remind you that God is with us. The whole idea is for us to be with God. Remember that.

B E L I E V I N G

"God"

Many of us are hard-pressed to define God beyond "superior being." That's not a bad attempt, actually. As United States Supreme Court Justice Potter Stewart famously allowed, with reference to a concept he could not define, "I know it when I see it."[3]

Those who truly *believe* will frequently "see" God in their daily lives—from witnessing acts of love and kindness by others, beauty in nature, or other arguably deistic manifestations. Non-believers are understandably unconvinced by that same evidence. As Father Stephen Palsa sagely observed in one of his many insightful sermons, "believing is seeing."

Many years ago, in the early morning of a winter's day, a more physically fit me (far more than I am currently) went for a run in Schenley Park. I was alone. The air was crisp in that quiet world covered with fresh-fallen snow. I padded down the path, and just as I reached a clearing in the woods, the sun came out. Its rays reflected brilliantly off so many thousands of snow crystals coating every twig, branch, and

---

3   Jacobellis v. Ohio, 378 U.S. 184 (1964) (concurring opinion). As a footnote reader, you're probably curious about what it was that Justice Stewart couldn't find words to define. Pornography. Though beyond the intended scope of this work, I want to suggest a means for dealing with temptations of the flesh. Develop a "trigger," whereby you always pray (for example, by saying a Hail Mary) upon first provocation of having an impure thought. This prayerful habit can take some time to develop. (It most certainly proved easier for this old man with prostate cancer.) Persevere! And if you're unfamiliar with the prayer I'm suggesting here, check out "Mary"—the penultimate section in this text—or find another prayer that will do. Saying a Hail Mary embarrasses me enough to stop before giving in to impure thoughts.

limb of the trees around that opening. The sight was captivating; it stopped me in my tracks. I said out loud, "God, it's you!" Believing is seeing.

That spontaneous utterance, provoked by the blinding beauty of a snowy morning? At best, it was an indirect manifestation. Had belief not already been in my heart,[4] I would have kept running without saying a word. Nice scenery.

While Christians have little difficulty *envisioning* God, that's because they're thinking of Christ. From the babe in a manger during Christmas to a fit-looking man with long, wavy hair and beard of respectable length, and of course the most oft-seen image of his crucifixion and death on a Calvary cross, images of Jesus abound. (There is objective, historic record of a charismatic "Pescador de Hombres"[5] on earth back then who recruited humble fishermen and others as apostles.) In western culture, his skin tends to be portrayed as considerably more white than a man of Jewish heritage living in the Middle East would actually have had. Inasmuch as Christ walked on earth more than 2,000 years ago, no one today can be heard to say, "He didn't look that way." He probably didn't, but looks don't matter—especially when it comes to God.

No religion can abide racism; God is love, racism a form of hate.

Our son Brendan brought me a gift from when he worked in Ethiopia: a painting of Mary as mother with her little child Jesus, rendered on leather. The faces depicted are all brown-skinned. As Brendan explains, this is because Christianity in Ethiopia significantly predates when fair-skinned missionaries preached and converted many in the rest of Africa (where images of a Caucasian Christ predominate). Skin color

---

4   Consider Michael Novak, *No One Sees God: The Dark Night of Atheists and Believers* (New York: Doubleday, 2008); "faith is the substance of things not seen" (Hebrews 11:1); and "No one has ever seen God . . ." (John 4:7–19). Following his Resurrection, Christ appeared to the apostles . . . except for Thomas, who remained in doubt until Christ's reappearance. When he actually touched Christ's wounds from crucifixion, Thomas became a believer, whereupon Christ said, "Blessed are those who have not seen and (yet) believe" (John 20:29).

5   "Pescador de Hombres," a soul-stirring hymn about Christ's fishing for those who would become apostles, authored by Cesario Gabarain and translated from the original Spanish into English by Fr. Willard Francis Jabusch, is in *Worship*, #760. In Luke 5:1–11, Jesus said to Simon Peter, who was a fisherman: "Do not be afraid; from now on you will be catching people."

shouldn't matter to us, whether it's in an image of Christ, a man or woman in the White House, or someone living in our neighborhood. "No race nor creed can love exclude/ If honored be God's name. . . ."[6] Reverend Martin Luther King got it right: the content of each individual's character is what really matters, or at least should.

I'm nonetheless pleased with the *champlevé* tabernacle door in the spectacularly beautiful little side chapel to the left of an enormous main altar area of my parish church (Sacred Heart, in Pittsburgh). Artistically representing the miracle involving five loaves and two fishes that Christ used to feed the multitudes, the door depicts Him and others with appropriately dark complexions. In the course of considering how things and persons *look*, earthlings may not realize just how severely hampered we are by our perceptive limitations. It is unsurprising that we have difficulty defining "God," inasmuch as none of our senses offers us any help. Even so, we can still believe in God. Because we humans learn so much from our senses of sight, smell, taste, touch, and hearing, however, we're prone to reject anything that cannot be grasped through them. It's unfortunate when such rejection happens, especially because in the process we're likely to rule out *believing*.

In his best-selling *Brief History of Time*, theoretical physicist Stephen Hawking refers to the "God particle." Sad to say, he later recanted by rejecting the notion of God in a subsequent book. His reason for doing so is based on thinking that gravity (without matter, or "stuff") affords an explanation of how the universe came into existence without any creative participation by a supreme being. (But then, where did gravity come from?) We ought not limit our perceptions of God to corporeal substances or physical phenomena. Let's discontinue the common practice of confining God to our physical world; better that we acknowledge and preserve obscurity of the "Am."

There may be folks who think that the speculations of some scientists, about origins of the universe or of human beings leave us without any reason to believe in God. But scientific hypotheses do not disprove God, and science never answers why

---

6   Hymn, "Where Charity and Love Prevail," (originally "*Ubi Caritas*"), translation by Omer Westendorf (1916–1997), verse 6, ©1960, World Library Publications, in *Worship*, #700. *See also*, Hymn, "In Christ There is No East or West," by William A. Dunkerly (1852–1941), alt. verse 3, final bars: "What e'er your race may be . . ./ Who serve each other in God's love/ Are surely kin to me," in *Worship*, #824.

there should be something rather than nothing. In sum, there is no reason for any believer to doubt God's existence on the basis of science.

At some point it's worth considering what part, if any, God plays *in your life*. Do you think it could be that "God" created our universe, with its vast complexity evolving over incomprehensible eons? Do *you think* anyone is "out there"? Might not God's fingerprints be found on many of the "coincidences" we experience? Does everything seem to make just a little bit more sense if we include God in the big picture? Even if you think science might be able to explain *how* we exist, it nonetheless seems worth asking: *why* do we exist?

"All others"

I'm most convinced by St. Thomas Aquinas' "uncaused cause" proof for the existence of God.[7] To me, that just makes sense, fed by my emotional feelings and backed up by daily observations of natural wonders. In total, Aquinas posits five arguments for believing in God, and I find them all to be persuasive. A present-day philosopher supplies us with *twenty* arguments![8] But don't mistake any of these many "proofs" as attempts to establish God as a matter of scientific fact; they are, each and every one, metaphysical reasons (reasons beyond empirical proof, that is) for **believing**. The inescapable element is *belief* in God, and I'm blessed to have an abundance of that.

Moreover, I personally believe that Christ existed. Jesus claimed often enough that it was He whom the Father sent, and He repeatedly reinforced that claim with miracles. So I don't think he was a blasphemer. But you don't have to agree with me. I might even be wrong (!), which takes me to my favorite cartoon from which to learn a valuable lesson.

Pictured are the gates into heaven. There are actually two portals. Next to one of them, a sign reads "For members of the one true religion." There's a long line of folks waiting to enter through that gate. Beside the other gate is a different sign, reading "All others." No one is seeking to enter there. A pair of cute little angels is standing alongside. "They just never seem to get it," says one of the cherubs to the other.[9]

Do *you* get it? Your beliefs are personal to you. The religion you choose to follow is not open to debate from others. By the same token, neither should we be intolerant of others' beliefs. "No one is excluded from the joy brought by the Lord."[10] Scarcely

---

7   St. Thomas Aquinas (1225–1274), Priest, Order of St. Dominic, in his *Summa Theologiae*, First Part, Question 2 (the existence of God), Article 3, offers five ways of proving God's existence. These are based on motion, nature of the efficient cause, possibility and necessity, the gradation to be found in things, and from the governance of the world by the "universal first cause." *See* Walter Farrell, OP, STD, STM, *A Companion to the Summa*: "They are inferential proofs, *a posteriori* proofs, inductions based on the facts of the sensible world and the first principles of reason." www.ewtn.com/library/ANSWERS/GODIS. Further, it must be acknowledged, Aquinas stated: "To one who has faith, no explanation is necessary. To one without faith, no explanation is possible."

8   See Peter J. Kreeft, "Twenty Arguments for the Existence of God," www.peterkreeft.com/topics-more/twenty-arguments-gods-existence.htm.

9   "Non Sequitur," by Wiley Miller (October 29, 2009), gocomics.com/nonsequitur, © '09 Wileyink, Inc.

10   Pope Paul VI, Apostolic Exhortation *Gaudete in Domino* (May 9, 1975), 22; AAS 67 (1975): 297.

anything could be more irreligious than disrespecting another's religion. Think of that cartoon and remember, the "other" folks just might be right!

We are talking about beliefs here, rather than scientific knowledge. Which is not to say that beliefs are weak tea in comparison with things we know about. I'm aware that all the objects around me now—pen, paper, cup of water, etc.—are made up of molecules. That's a scientific fact, and I take it to be true. But the Last Supper, when Jesus presented the unleavened bread as "my body" and wine as "my blood"? I'm convinced that all happened. And my convictions more than hold their own against the molecular make-up of things, which I respect as established science.

✦

Everyone who believes in the existence of God, and each individual who is at all religious, formulates their own outlook. Many are blessed to have been influenced by parents who brought them up in a given faith tradition. Others, with the help of God, find their own way. At the same time, each well-established religion promulgates its own tenets of faith. For Catholics as well as most other Christians, these are neatly contained in the Nicene Creed (see also the Apostles' Creed), which is prayed aloud during most Sunday Masses. Of course, those who follow a given religion are expected to accept its articles while adopting its practices; we don't get to choose, as if from a menu, one tenet from column A, another from column B, etc.

✦

Father Joseph Freedy said St. Valentine's Day (2017) Mass at 8:15 a.m. in St. Paul Cathedral in Pittsburgh this morning. Familiar Gospel verses from Genesis had been read during the past ten days, and this morning's involved Noah. Father Freedy's homily urged trust in God's love: "Do not leave the ark, even during stormy times," he counseled, while drawing a connection between Noah's craft and today's Catholic Church. I could not help but think back to an offshore sailing trip with our friend Jay Gowell and his wife Liz. Jay is a former student of mine, but far more importantly he was a professional sailor before going to law school. He had recently purchased *Southerly*, a seventy-foot aluminum ketch lying in Fort Lauderdale, Florida. Our five-member crew was to sail her up to Rhode Island. A steamer-trunk-sized canister contained our life raft, secured on deck to one of *Southerly*'s lifeline stanchions by braided steel cable. In worst case conditions (*Southerly*'s sinking), the safety device called a "hammer" would sever that steel cable with an explosive charge triggered by water pressure. If the big boat went several feet below the surface, the hammer would explode, releasing our life raft to bob-up to the surface, for us to board in relative safety. An EPIRB (emergency position-indicating radio beacon) would supposedly guide a helicopter to our position, which, for most of this voyage, was east of the Gulf Stream. Father Freedy was correct: it's a bad idea to leave the ark...which is to say the church. A minor explosion was prerequisite to our leaving *Southerly* in favor of a small life raft, and we would never do so voluntarily. Neither should anyone depart the church on grounds of personal disagreement. We all need help to guide us "o'er life's tempestuous sea." Try your best to ride-out any squalls by staying with the church.

Any number of "hot button" issues could conceivably cause a fissure to develop between an otherwise faithful Catholic and the church. In that event, we need to ask ourselves whether the church's positions *inconvenience* us. Catholics as well as other Christians—the members of all other religions, for that matter—do not have the prerogative of navigating around inconvenient tenets of their faith. We all have to abide, to the best of our abilities; prayer coupled with deep love of God is the very best means of getting there.

The relationship each of us forms with God is unique and intensely personal. (The prospect of others' sharing your concept of "God" in all respects may be about as likely as finding two identical snowflakes!) During the course of our faith journey, however, we have to put aside personal differences. Take, for example, Simon the Zealot and Matthew the tax-collector, both of whom Christ recruited as apostles. Their political positions could hardly have been farther apart or more irreconcilable—what with Simon the Zealot's affiliation with Jews opposed to the Romans, and Matthew's collecting taxes to support the Roman Empire! Yet, they followed Christ with full resolve, as we too must do—even in the face of possible disagreements with our church, its clergy, or its hierarchy.

✦

Always try to maintain your personal relationship with God through prayer—including conversational ones in addition to those prayers available "off the shelf," that you've held in memory for years and years. Talk with God *every day*, and *more than once* each day! I'm not assigning you a task here; I hold no such authority. But there's a path for reaching your joyful life with God, and it starts with these daily conversations. Have faith. Doubt not.

As I prune the phrases,
       leaving but one word,
Assembling thoughts in stages . . .

*Searching for the **perfect prayer**,*
My hope is God will find me there.

"What counts are thoughts . . .
       not words that ought,"
Said He, correcting me.
"I love all prayers, from everyone,
What 'ere their language be."

I promptly stopped
       my fruitless search,
And began to say,
       "Hello" to God while on my way
       through each and every day . . .
Admire his creations
       (they are God's handiwork),
And say how thankful I've become,
       now praying is less work!

Participation

The earliest church-going experiences I recall date back to Saint Peter's grammar school days on Staten Island, New York. I sang as a soprano in the all-male choir, populated mostly by older gentlemen with much deeper voices. There was also a church-based "Blanket Club" in which my mother played an active role, a church-school-related "Mother's Club" of which she served as president for a while, and most likely Bingo (or is this just stereotyping on my part?).

As my pastor here in Pittsburgh, Father Robert Grecco, has observed from the pulpit, back in those "old days" the church was a local venue for many social and religious activities. I met Bishop Fulton J. Sheen when he came to speak at St. Peter's Church. Thanks to his weekly television show, "Life is Worth Living," Bishop Sheen was popular well beyond Catholic circles. I thought he had to be the most charismatic man on earth! (At a recent black-tie event here in Pittsburgh, I was sitting next to a highly regarded local, non-Catholic architect who happened to mention Bishop Sheen. He, too, had years ago met Bishop Sheen in person and made the very same assessment of him.) Much has changed since fifty-plus years ago.[11] Not many churches today function as a hub of community activity the way they used to, and Masses are not so well attended as they once were, either.

On the positive side, virtually everyone present at any given Catholic Mass these days will partake of the Holy Eucharist. When I was young, only slightly more than half of Mass attendees might receive. Perhaps this change can be attributed to replacing the obligation of fasting from midnight with the easier requirement of fasting for at least one hour before receiving Communion.

At the same time, it is disturbing to note, confessions (the Sacrament of Reconciliation) seem to occur with less frequency. From what once was prevalent as a near-weekly event (in an era when "a month since my last confession" sounded terribly self-incriminating), we would appear to have *either* come to conduct our lives more free from sin *or* redefined more narrowly what we consider to be sinful. Which of those alternatives do *you* think better explains the fall-off in confessions? I suspect

---

11   *See* Charles E. Zech, Mary L. Gantier, Mark M. Gray, Jonathan L. Wiggins, and Thomas P. Gaunt, *Catholic Parishes of the 21st Century* (Oxford: Oxford University Press, 2017).

it's the latter; it seems that we may have legitimized heretofore untoward behavior and perhaps lost our sense of guilt. As Father Grecco stated during his homily at yesterday afternoon's Vigil Mass (July 22, 2017), "Unfortunately, what was evil years ago may be tolerated now, but it is still wrong."

Irving Berlin's once-playful lyrics about ragtime dancing in 1911, "Everybody's doin' it, doin' it, doin' it," became bastardized in the 1960s as moral justification for whatever popular behavioral practices were then the norm. In a similar vein are Cole Porter's lyrics to his 1934 composition, "Anything Goes." *The crowd* cannot give us cover today from behavior that remains confessional. Contemporary social practices ought not be accepted as setting moral standards, no matter how prevalent or popular such practices might be; it is an unsupportable rationalization to conflate them with *morality*. For illustrative purposes, consider prescription opioids—drugs which, when limited in application to instances of true need (as they're intended, to suppress pain), serve a useful purpose. But as prescribing them became more widespread, illicit usage increased, and an epidemic developed. Trends are inevitable, and a feeling of security results from adopting normative behaviors—including medical treatment options currently popular among physicians.[12] We have to be wary of assuming contemporary societal practices are *per se* acceptable as a moral matter. Quite obviously, that assumption won't always be correct; let your conscience (informed by the Magisterium) be your guide.

✦

Our blink in time on earth is supposed to be spent loving God and all of our neighbors at least as much as we love ourselves. We have to make an earnest attempt, on a regular basis, to confess all else. I'm sure that if a very important guest were coming to visit, you would make every effort to clean and straighten-up your house. There is no more important guest than Jesus Christ, who comes to us in the Holy Eucharist, so *clean up* as thoroughly as you can.

---

12   The heart of the matter, unnecessary prescribing, is compounded by opioid drug manufacturers' payments (akin to unethical "kickbacks") totaling more than $46 million to 68,000-plus doctors during twenty-nine months: <Opioid makers made payments to one in 12 U.S. doctors>

See also Anna Lembke, MD, *Drug Dealer, MD: How Doctors Were Duped, Patients Got Hooked, and Why It's So Hard to Stop* (Baltimore: Johns Hopkins University Press, 2016).

I've gone through stages when it felt too shameful to confess the same sins as last week. After passing up the Sacrament of Reconciliation, I would tend to add insult to injury by skipping Sunday Mass (rather than publicly admit to mortal sin by crouching in the pew during Communion). Don't fall prey to this downward spiral; it just keeps getting worse. Never be afraid to confess. The priest hearing your confession won't be shocked by however badly you may have behaved. Heed the words of Pope Francis: "His mercy is infinitely greater than our sins."

By the way, the Catholic Act of Contrition—which should not be reserved for confessional circumstances—expresses two quite different motivations. Dreading the loss of heaven and pains of hell is one, but the top-shelf choice is "because I have offended Thee, my God, who art all good and deserving of all my love." The latter, being more laudable, is sometimes called "perfect contrition."

I know well how difficult it is to confess sins. Do it anyway! Realize that your bad feelings are a manifestation of guilt for having sinned. That means you'll make a *good confession*! After confessing your sins and doing penance, you become entitled to enjoy the most intimate time with God by receiving the Holy Eucharist in Communion.

Thus do we arrive at the "great divide" between Catholicism on the one side, and Christianity in general on the other. At every Mass, bread and wine are offered up to God and consecrated. This is not merely a *re-enactment* of the Last Supper. The priest actually replicates what Jesus did on that occasion; speaking as a direct disciple of Christ, he pronounces, "this is my body . . ." over the bread, and "this is my blood . . ." over the wine. There's a sort of fillip, "Do this in memory of me," that Protestants take as a directive to *re-enact*—which is not quite equivalent to *replicating* exactly what Christ did. When a Catholic receives Communion, the server says, "Body of Christ," and the communicant responds "Amen," which means "so it is" or "so be it." This brief exchange confirms Catholics' belief in transubstantiation, a *sacred mystery*. This is considered a miracle; "the highest unity in the Divine order is the unity of the soul and Christ in communion."[13]

✦

---

13   Archbishop Fulton J. Sheen, *Life of Christ* (1954, reprinted Mansfield Centre, CT: Martino Publishing, 2016), 401–402.

As usual, we humans tend to take stock of what our senses tell us, above all else. Because *accidentals* (i.e., observable physical properties) of the consecrated bread and wine remain, some Catholics find "transubstantiation" to pose a believability challenge. Make no mistake about what Christ meant when saying "this is my body"; doctrinally, the Holy Eucharist is not merely symbolic. Christ knew full well how to use symbolism, and did so earlier during that same evening when he stooped to wash the feet of his apostles: "I have given you a model to follow." (NABRE John 13:15. In place of "model," other translations use "pattern" or "example.") Then Christ said, "As I, your teacher, have washed your feet, so must you be willing to serve in my name." In contrast, accounts of the Last Supper are bereft of any language akin to that which accompanied the washing of feet when Christ later pronounced over the bread and wine, "this is my body," and "this is my blood." While not a biblical scholar, I would argue that the language Christ used when washing the apostles' feet indicates *that* to have been a symbolic act, whereas the lack of similar-type language when consecrating the bread and wine supports taking it literally—which comports with the Catholic Church's view on transubstantiation.

Christ declared, when teaching in the Synagogue at Capernaum (well before the Last Supper), "I am the bread of life." He said this twice (John 6:35 and 48 NIV) before explicitly connecting "the bread" as a reference to his own body: "This bread is my flesh, which I will give for the life of the world ... [and] unless you eat the flesh of the Son of Man and drink his blood, you have no life in you. Whoever eats my flesh and drinks my blood has eternal life, and I will raise up at the last day. For my flesh is real food and my blood is real drink." (John 6:51, 53–55 NIV).[14] Were the Holy Eucharist to involve no more than a wafer of unleavened bread and optional sip of wine, the following opprobrium from I Corinthians 11:27–29 would certainly seem excessive: "Whoever, therefore, eats the bread or drinks

At first blush,
Love invited,
"Break bread
with me to see
my Father," so
I did ~ and the
rest is . . . eternity.

---

14   *Cf* John 6:51 (USCCB): "I am the living bread that came down from heaven; whoever eats this bread will live forever; and the bread that I will give is my flesh for the life of the world."

the cup of the Lord in an unworthy manner will be answerable for the body and blood of the Lord."

From Holy Thursday to the feast of Corpus Christi, transubstantiation of the bread and wine is underscored, with the Eucharist being celebrated as the body and blood of Jesus Christ. There's no greater nourishment for the soul than this.

L E A V I N G

Drift

Most of my life has been lived proximate to expanses of water. Many were tidal. Small dinghies and rowing prams are ubiquitous in those surroundings. Whenever in the water (rather than resting in a rack, on land), these minor craft are held fast by a modest length of line called a "painter," hitched to a dock or mooring. If not properly tied, the painter will gradually come undone. As tides alternately slacken and pull, the painter will ever so gently be coaxed free, leaving the little boat adrift. *Algarete!*

Prayer works a lot like that rope painter by holding our tender souls fast to God. We need to make sure it doesn't loosen, lest we drift away. That's what happened to me.

It just happened. There was never any resolve on my part to bid adieu to God or the Catholic Church. In retrospect, the experience seems to fall within the time-honored notion of having occurred "in the normal course of human events." I just drifted away. It was gradual. Mostly unconscious. Hardly inexorable except when viewed in hindsight—only after I came to possess some awareness of where I had ended up. Fortunately, that's not where (or when) my life ended with God.

✦

Indifference induces drift. As a long-time teacher I can tell you there's nothing sadder to say about any student than that he or she is "indifferent." Learning is most unlikely to happen in the face of indifference. My effort in the classroom is to *engage* all students by showing them my enthusiasm for the subject so that their minds don't drift.

Indifference is intolerable. Those are strong words with which you may not altogether agree, but I really want you to give them some serious thought.

During the classic children's play, Peter Pan (which succeeds in touching many a grown-up's heart), there's a moment when Tinker Bell could die. The lovable fairy's fate rests in the hands of the audience. Literally. Audience applause saves Tinker Bell! Indifference can be deadly—not just to Tinker Bell, but in your life here on earth, and still more importantly to your immortal soul.

Take a moment and think about the folks whom you like most. I doubt that group is heavily populated by individuals who harbor a "ho hum" attitude. With whom would you most enjoy sharing a meal, or watching a sports event, or conversing? While the personality profiles of those individuals may well differ from one another—depending upon what you were planning on doing together—it's likely that all of them would share with you a common level of interest and *involvement*. I hope that these situations serve to heighten your awareness of the possibly poisonous effects of indifference.

It is impermissible to be indifferent toward God.

It's perfectly acceptable to feel indifferent about whether to have pie or ice cream for dessert! But a savvy coach might actually bench the best athlete on a squad if that player's head isn't in the game. Lacking a significant level of involvement, or commitment, are kindred to being indifferent, which can easily offset a wealth of raw talent.

It is simply impermissible to be indifferent toward God. If you've ever admired passionately committed folks with "a fire in the belly," why not consider starting a fire in *your* heart, fueled by love of God? Your initial decision to turn toward God will be the kindling, and your determination will be the spark. Just start gradually, by saying a "Good morning, God" prayer at the start of your day, and a "Good night" prayer in the evening. Converse with God by previewing your day at the start (asking for understanding, patience, and wisdom for the times when you anticipate needing such help). Then, at night, review the day with God, giving thanks, making apologies—whatever seems fitting. As these practices become routine, slowly add similar moments of prayer during the rest of the day. Try putting God into your daily life like this and you will banish indifference forever. Drift no more. Once you possess a level of conscious awareness and regular involvement with God, your life will never again be hollow at its core, and you'll likely feel joy as never before.

Smoking

Roger had a brand new car, and besides, he loved to golf. But it was late winter in Pittsburgh. Roger's law school classmate, Bob Lichtenstein, and his wife Sandy wanted to spend their Spring Break week in the sun. The three of them had found a couple of inexpensive rooms on Grand Bahama Island off the coast of Florida, and the airfare from Miami was only $38. Their plan was to start driving on Friday, non-stop, to Miami.

On the Monday before, Bob poked his head into my office to ask if I'd like to come along. I would have to do a fair share of the driving, as Sandy was unfamiliar with the still-stiff stick-shift transmission in Roger's Buick Opel, but then get to spend the next week living in another culture, in another country. In addition to my liking Bob (a brilliant student), his pitch sounded pretty appealing.

I went, unaware that all three of them smoked . . . like chimneys. I didn't, and disliked breathing second-hand smoke. But by the Carolinas I was bumming their cigarettes.

I bought a carton during the homeward-bound leg a week later.

When taking the last pack of Marlboros from that depleted carton stashed in my desk back at work in Pittsburgh, I thought, "Need to buy cigarettes." It was my first moment of conscious awareness that I was a smoker. But I knew it wasn't for me. Having fought against asthma while growing up, I really didn't like what this brief foray into smoking was doing to me, and so the nascent habit ended before it took hold. It had just happened—I drifted into smoking. I was carried along by the current of my three young friends—who offered absolutely no encouragement for me to take up smoking. By close analogy to this experience, it's quite possible for us to be unaware of having changed direction away from God.

We need to look in the mirror and ask whether we're drifting away from God.

Because drifting is by and large unconscious, our behavior patterns can form before we even arrive at a state of awareness about them. If we are fortunate enough to recognize where we're headed before those patterns become established in a deeply engrained way, quitting can come easy. That's why introspection is important, the sort of introspection that comes from regularly examining our conscience. We need to look in that mirror and question whether we're drifting away from God.

Musical Chairs

Anyone who has played the game of musical chairs knows how to arrange things. You need a source of music, typically one that can be interrupted with ease, without any warning. And chairs. The usual set-up is to place the chairs side-by-side, facing in alternate directions. Participants stand around the chairs, which are one fewer in number than the players. When the music begins, everyone proceeds to march around the line of chairs. At any given moment, one is either adjacent to a chair seat, or next to the back of a chair. As everyone knows, the music is destined to stop, and at that moment each participant must sit down. There being a limited supply of chairs, someone will be left standing. That person is "out." Unlike most battles, where the last one standing is victorious, the object here is to be the last one sitting!

Musical chairs can serve as a handy metaphor to help us live a holy life. Like the old saw of biblical origin, "we know not the day or the hour," the music can stop at any moment, without warning. If we want a seat reserved for us in heaven, it's necessary to be ready *all the time* for the music to stop.

As the game of musical chairs proceeds along, its analogy to our faith journey seems to grow evermore strong. What does it matter that you had a seat when last the music stopped, if the game is ongoing? "Let a man be ever so holy now, he may fall away . . . as grace is no pledge of perseverance," John Henry Newman warns us, for "those who have prophesied in God's Name may *afterwards* fall from God , and lose their souls."[15]

Lest the musical chairs image strike you as too childish or overly simplistic, I offer the following alternative. My body has come to resemble a damaged timepiece that's running slow; cancer and the medical means of impeding its progress have damaged me physically. Besides, I'm not getting any younger. At some point, real time will come to coincide with this old- and slow-timer. In a manner of speaking, my time will then be *up*. No greater level of predictability inures to me by virtue of being super-annuated or having cancer (though the inevitability of life's end might seem a bit

---

15   John Henry Newman (1801–1890), *Discourses Addressed to Mixed Congregations* (1849), republished with introduction by James Tolhurst (Notre Dame, Indiana: University of Notre Dame, 2003).

closer in time for me). The fact remains that none of us knows *when*, and that is my point: *semper paratus*!

In the same vein, from the New Testament, is Matthew 24:44:

Be sure of this: if the master of the house had known of the hour of night when the thief was coming, he would have stayed awake and not let his house be broken into. So too, you also must be prepared, for at an hour you do not expect, the Son of Man will come.

✦

Once you leave God, an obliviousness obviously sets in toward any concern about being in "the state of grace." By way of contrast, anyone who remains mindful about "loss of heaven and pains of hell" hasn't drifted so far away. A change of course by that person ought be relatively easy to make.

Once you leave God, your church, or religion, an obliviousness sets in toward concerns about being in "the state of grace."

But what about those who've drifted farther? When I was a little boy, beautiful books were given to me at Christmas every year by a friend of my parents, Florence Ames Wood. One of the titles was *All Dogs Go to Heaven*, a sentiment with which I agree! (As one wag put it: all dogs go to heaven simply because they've earned it by having to deal with humans during their entire lives!) I'm skeptical in the extreme about whether all *human beings* are going to heaven; and I definitely worry about my own qualifications. A concern about what the after-life holds in store can presage a course-correction by those who drift away. But many of those who drift afar may not think about their after-life, if indeed they believe in one.

In his book *The Aristos*, author John Fowles maintains that those who do not believe in a life after death will generally comport themselves more considerately toward their fellow man than a religious-minded person might. For example, Fowles postulates two truck drivers, each hauling explosive cargo. He suggests that the "no after-life" driver will proceed more cautiously—precisely because this is all there is.[16] Arguably, if Fowles is correct, we need only be concerned here with the other driver (who believes in an after-life), but I think Fowles is mistaken.

I take issue with Fowles' apparent disbelief in an afterlife. An afterlife is incorporated by virtually all religions into their doctrinal tenets of faith. Of course, that doesn't *prove* anything, so perhaps an analogy to the "climate change" (aka "global warming") debate might help. A preponderance of opinion in the scientific community considers climate change to pose a real threat to our planet.[17] And yet there are also deniers, who scoff at the notion that mankind is either causing or at least contributing to climate change. If we take no action to reduce or mitigate its ill effects, however, we could pass the point of no return. Then it will be too late to deal with the threat effectively or adequately. Whichever side of the debate is correct, industrialized nations could foster a cleaner earth's atmosphere by reducing carbon emissions and curbing greenhouse gasses.

Belief in God and an afterlife (though not scientifically-backed propositions as is climate change) should encourage peace. (I'm banking on the notion that God disfavors hatred and wars; Jesus is often referred to as the "Prince of Peace," after all.) Thus, by putting stock in the existence of an afterlife—just as by accepting the hypothesis of climate change—we will stand to benefit regardless of whether global warming *and* an afterlife are *both* just a bunch of *hooey*.

Returning to Fowles' tale of two truck drivers: in concluding that the "this life is all there is" driver will be the more cautious, Fowles fails to consider *Judgment Day*— an inextricable ingredient of believing in an afterlife. Since those who believe in an afterlife expect it to last for eternity, there's enormously more at stake for the driver who believes. Fowles' logic is flawed.

✦

---

16   John Fowles, *The Aristos* (New York: Little Brown, 1964), 29, paragraph numbered 33.

17   "A very solid scientific consensus indicates that we are presently witnessing a disturbing warming of the climate system." *Laudato Sí*, on care for our common home, Encyclical Letter of Pope Francis (Libreria Editrice Vaticana, Vatican City, 2015), 20. *See also* Global Climate Change: A Plea for Dialogue, Prudence, and the Common Good, U.S. Conf. of Catholic Bishops, <http://store.usccbb.org/global-climate-change-a-plea-for-dialog.p/5.431.htm#>. WRsvS4nbMbg.email>; Norman Myers and Jennifer Kent, *The New Consumers: The Influence of Affluence on the Environment* (Washington: Island Press, 2004).

The objective, of which we must remain mindful, is to have a place secured in heaven for whenever the music stops. Striving for an eternal reward is but one motivation that can be posed. There's also the *loss* of heaven and fears of hell, as well as the pure motive of avoiding actions (or inaction) offensive to God, by living a life that will be pleasing to God. Any or all of these could encourage—yea, conceivably even cause—one who has drifted away to reverse course and come back.

Horse

A scriptural story familiar to many involves the Hebrew, Saul of Tarsus, who was unseated from his horse—as if struck by lightning—while riding on Damascus Road. A voice with no visible source spoke to him as he lay on the ground. The voice expressed displeasure with Saul's persecution of Christians. Thereupon did Saul convert. With his name changed to Paul, he served as a witness, preacher, and teacher on behalf of Joshua the Christ. (This is recounted in The Acts of the Apostles, written in Greek by Luke: Acts 9:1–8; 22:3–10; and 26:12–19.) Along the way, Paul enlisted Timothy and Titus to help spread the Word, and they, in turn, both became saints as well!

I've never even sat on a horse, and there was no corollary in my life to Paul's experience. I cannot offer you even a metaphoric "horse" from which to fall and thereupon return to God. Unlike the story of Saul/Paul, I'm unable to recount in great detail what it was that turned me around, but here's what happened.

There was a day, during that period when Catholics are charged to perform their "Easter Duty" by going to confession (the Sacrament of Reconciliation). I had decided that it was high time for me to confess my sins and receive Communion the next day, on Easter Sunday. Since it was Saturday, the usual day when confessions are heard throughout the year, this seemed like a sensible plan. But St. Paul Cathedral was deserted! How could this be? I checked every one of the confessional areas around the church; all of them were dark and empty…which was unnerving. Then I spotted a cleaning person, who I asked about confessions. "Oh, there are none being heard today. It's Holy Saturday," she explained. My mind couldn't process this; I'd been away long enough to have forgotten about the Holy Triduum. Those are the three most solemn days in the liturgical year, and not just for Catholics but for Christians in general. Maundy Thursday is when Christ and the twelve apostles gathered for supper (the Last Supper). Though Jesus was God-made-man, he was humble, particularly on this occasion by washing his apostles' feet. (This was on the night before Judas betrayed Christ.) Good Friday is when Christ was crucified and died for us; afternoon services solemnly commemorate this. On Holy Saturday, Catholic churches usually go dark until nighttime—no confessions, no Vigil Mass that would count for Easter Sunday. I had to go find a priest, as my feelings of anguish were growing.

I walked over to the front entry of St. Paul Cathedral's parish house in the Oakland section of Pittsburgh. (Coincidentally, it was St. Paul who implored, "Now is a very acceptable time" [2 Corinthians 6:2], but those words weren't on my mind; only my sins were.) Upon being welcomed into the parish house, I expressed a desire to confess my sins. Soon thereafter I was introduced to Father Kim Shrek, who heard my confession face-to-face, in his office. This arrangement made the experience all the more awkward and embarrassing for me.

I had to go find a priest, as my feelings of anguish were growing.

Penitents in the Sacrament of Reconciliation are not necessarily seen by the priest; there is typically a screen between them and the priest. Having undergone a confession where the priest knew who I was, my anonymous confessions following that experience with Father Shrek seemed less tension-filled. Even so, they remain scary whenever the wheels come off and there's something serious to confess.

Pouring-out my soul to Father Shrek was most painful; it brought tears of sorrow, in repentance. I don't know why my turnaround occurred that day. I only recall feeling an overdue need. No horse, but probably a voice.

Just how "overdue" was that event? My wife recalls taking our children to St. Paul Cathedral for Easter Mass in previous years. I wasn't with them, despite my being a Catholic, while Eliza is Presbyterian. She couldn't help wondering why they were attending "my" church instead of nearby Shadyside Presbyterian, where she's a member. Does sheer embarrassment becloud my memory? I have no recollection whatsoever of the Easter(s) my wife recounts. Not that I doubt her one bit. While Eliza claims to have a poor memory, she doesn't in fact. But even if her head were a sieve, you have to think this father's absenting himself from Mass with his family is pathetic enough to stick in her mind (as well as—worse yet—our children's). "Overdue" hardly begins to capture my delinquency.

RETURNING

It's generally thought that fear of death will serve as a sure-fire incentive for sinners to repent. Maybe so, but not in my experience.

Cancer Causes

I was familiar with the oft-heard warning sign of cancer—a lump or thickening in the breast or elsewhere—when this happened:

One evening, a hem around the neck of my tee-shirt tickled a spot near the left-side collar bone. I scratched at it lightly, and felt something. Moments later, I looked in my bathroom mirror but saw nothing suspicious there. Then I felt for and found a marble-sized, sub-dermal something or other. Hmmm.

Saturday morning, as our senior-aged running group began slogging down a Schenley Park trail, I told Dr. Kevin Gibson about my little lump. He stopped, felt it with his skilled hands, and said that a needle aspiration would be necessary in order for anyone to make a reliable, professional diagnosis.A few days later, my nervous morning of being looked at by diagnostic specialists culminated with the needle aspiration Kevin had predicted. (Though he specializes in pulmonology, Kevin never ceases to amaze me with the breadth of his medical expertise.) By the time an aspiration finally occurred, I had been under observation for hours—long enough that an apologetic public announcement was made to a waiting room full of other patients, as well as my wife. Eliza heard it; I did not. We went home without knowing anything more, except that this morning's investigative medical crew had apparently been "concerned."

My primary care physician (PCP) interrupted me during the following Saturday afternoon's pachysandra planting session. He phoned to tell me that my lump was cancerous. I had Hodgkin's Disease. Bad news. The "good news," he told me, was that if I had to make a choice, Hodgkin's was among the most curable of all cancers. That was heartening to hear. Even so, my preferred choice would far and away have been "it's benign." And so I returned to planting pachysandra—but now on four-inch centers. Before that call from my PCP, I was placing the rooted cuttings six inches apart. My horizon seemed suddenly to have moved closer.

On the basis of a PET/CT scan, I was found to be Stage 3-a. Dr. Stanley Marks, the oncologist to whom I was blessed to be referred, put me on a nine-month program of intravenous chemotherapy. His offices included an expansive room ringed with reclining lounge chairs; this was where patients received their chemo treatments. Positioned adjacent to each recliner was a metal "tree" from which the recumbent patient's plastic bags of chemotherapy drugs hung. The first time we ever saw all this, Eliza and I were shocked by the eerie otherworldly setting. We were also surprised that so many people were being treated. It was there that four chemo drugs (referred to in the trade as "ABVD") were dripped into my veins every other week. A few months later, I had no eyebrows, eyelashes, or hair anywhere. And some of the foods I had liked the most became impossible for me to eat. (Having even less willpower than usual while undergoing chemo, I turned into an ice cream junkie along the way.)

Not very long after my chemotherapy regimen began, a former student, John Iurlano, called. He asked if I liked lasagna. Caught by surprise, I hesitated. "There's traditional cheese, sausage, and seafood," he added. Sausage sounded good to me. A few days later he appeared at our front door with a magnificent Pyrex casserole full, that he had prepared for us. This would have been generous enough, but John shrugged-off our effusive thanks by explaining that he had simply doubled the recipe . . . because his wife Ann was fighting cancer, and he had assumed cooking duties during her battle. In due course over the ensuing weeks John followed up with traditional cheese, and then seafood lasagna. Chemotherapy can wreck one's appetite and cause nausea to boot, but the main ingredient in John's lasagna was love—which remains readily digestible and most nourishing. Both Ann and I survived on it!

Chemotherapy is cumulative. Its effects build. There came to be nights when my mind harbored real doubts about surviving until dawn. I left the little light on my bedside table burning.

None of this brought me back to God.

Clot Effects

I had to be hospitalized for a blood clot during the course of my chemotherapy. While clots are not uncommon among chemo patients, mine was of the dangerous deep vein thrombosis (DVT) variety. Efforts to dissolve it with Coumadin, a blood thinner that's also used as rat poison (the rodents bleed to death), kept me hospitalized beyond the scheduled date for my next round of chemotherapy. I began thinking of myself as a one-man triage challenge to hospital staff: they had to decide between dealing with the clot or the cancer. My bet was that cancer posed a more dire threat, so I demanded to be released from the hospital in order to resume chemotherapy. This was a quest that would smack of insanity under any other circumstances!

While lying in the hospital bed waiting for clot-risks to subside, I declined a visiting priest's offer to hear my confession: "No, thanks." Whatever possessed me to turn down that priestly offer? I have no idea. Perhaps it was the daunting prospect of looking my confessor in the eye. (This was years before I met with Father Kim Shrek.) Until then, during every other time I received the Sacrament of Reconciliation, the priest had been separated from me by a screen. The difference, in that hospital room context, may well have spooked me.

Recovering from a long-term drift isn't necessarily easy. Even in the face of an inducement coupled with an invitation, such as I experienced, it need not happen. That's free will. To change direction and recover from drifting away, we need to become more purposeful about where we're headed in life. I squandered this opportunity.

✦

Some years went by before another blood clot developed. I had learned from experience what a deep vein thrombosis felt like, though, and one fine day the feeling was there, in my left leg. A strange telephonic exchange with my PCP's office ensued: "You probably don't get many calls from patients who tell you their diagnosis, but I have a clot." "You have to go to Shadyside Hospital, or else come in to see the doctor right away." "No can do, I have to teach a class." With threats of dire consequences if I refused, the nurse insisted that I come to the office, and promised me an expedited visit if I would do so. With a flare for the dramatic, my doctor sent me to the pharmacy across the street from his office with a prescription, and instructions to take a double-dose right then and there before returning. While I was doing that, he arranged for me to be seen by a cardiology specialist at Shadyside Hospital. I made it to class. (Teaching/learning tax law is life or death, you realize.) It wasn't a particularly ominous-looking clot; everyone figured it would soon dissolve.

Little more than a week later I awoke with disturbingly dysfunctional legs. Eliza called for an ambulance despite my protestations that she could just as well drive me to the hospital. She was downstairs welcoming an EMS crew into our home when I lost consciousness while standing unsteadily next to our bed. Everyone heard the fall, whereupon things reportedly got fairly thrilling. One EMS guy tore open my shirt while another urged me to wake up 'cause my wife was worried. I slept through. Eventually they carried me downstairs on a litter: a harrowing descent (by which point I was unfortunately awake) that caused me to toss my cookies! The ambulance ride to Shadyside Hospital was likewise punctuated by repeated spurts of reverse peristalsis. At the hospital, it was soon discovered that my clot had become bigger. Then it came to light that I had inherited a blood-clotting disorder: a gene mutation called "Factor V (five) Leiden." This presumably came from my mother, who I recall being concerned about a DVT for much of her life. Another, considerably less scientific reason for suspecting that my mother was the source of this mutation: her nickname was "Gene"!

✦

On several occasions over the years, while we were all vacationing in the southeastern Massachusetts shore town of Marion, I'd made pilgrimages to a manufacturing facility in nearby Wareham, called "Factory Five." They produce the components for mechanically-inclined individuals to assemble spitting-image replicas of the famed Shelby Cobra street-legal race car. And now, at long last, I nearly had my very own Factor[y] Five! Oh well, given my driving history, overpopulated as it is with "close calls," I'm doubtless better off living with a gene mutation than courting death behind the wheel of a Cobra whose stampeding herd of horses under the hood wouldn't wait for my aging reflexes to catch up! Awareness that we don't always get what we want (something I picked up from Mick Jagger) shouldn't keep us from praying. It is by no means a rationalization to accept that God knows far better than we do what's best for each of us. The providential hand of God guides us always, albeit at times to places we would rather not go. Anyone who thinks this disproves God's existence must regard life on earth as our "eternal reward"!

✦

The day after my admittance to Shadyside Hospital, Dr. James O'Toole proposed to install a small wire "parasol" intravenously, to interdict my blood clot in the event it became migratory. This procedure really scared me. (You cannot *imagine* just how much of an understatement that is!)

Shortly before I was wheeled from my hospital room on the way to that science-fiction-like surgical insertion, I noticed a priest look in—but he saw that a lot was going on, and left. During the next couple of terrifying hours I kept thinking about how much more important that priest probably was than all those doctors who were taking my life into their hands, inserting that innocent-looking little wire.

✦

What about my thinking wistfully of that priest who had appeared at my hospital room right before I was wheeled out for a surreal surgery? I certainly didn't pick up on it at the time, but that's apparently when I began to turn around! Later, when he came back and we actually met, Father Sodini mentioned that daily Mass was celebrated in the hospital chapel. I never went. Turning around is one thing; coming back is yet another—and that takes substantial time.

Turning around is one thing; coming back is yet another— and that takes substantial time.

I was back in my room, with the wire "parasol" now safely ensconced, when Father Sodini returned to visit with me. I began to recount what I had just undergone. He listened politely for a brief while, before letting me know that it's a quite common procedure. With that, I could not help thinking to myself, "you mean, I said all of those prayers for *nothing*?!!"

The prayers we say are never wasted. After all, I survived a surgical procedure involving an incision in my neck, the opening of a vein, and the insertion of a thin-metal-wire "parasol" pushed down that blood-tube until it was just where the medical crew wanted. The surgeon does this by watching a screen where goings-on inside the patient appear "live" (preferably), and once the parasol is in place, they somehow *deploy* the tiny umbrella so that its ribs spread open inside the vein. To this day, years later, I still feel the fear induced by that surgery. (Memories of it returned earlier today during our regular Saturday morning old-timer's jog in Schenley Park, but for the first time . . . I laughed. The umbrella reminded me of that famous movie scene starring Pittsburgh's own Gene Kelly, "Singing in the *Vein*"!) Wouldn't you know, that clot never budged! The entire parasol-install procedure proved to have been . . . for *nothing*! Even so, my prayers were nonetheless worthwhile.

At home afterward, I had to use a walker to get around. Dr. O'Toole ordered me to walk, so laps around the dining table alternating with round-trips about the first floor of our home became a daily regimen. Memories of having once been a marathon runner haunted me. After almost six weeks, it was time for the parasol to be removed. Remaining awake enough under local anesthetic, I heard the surgeon exclaim when, on the very first try, he hooked onto an infinitesimally small loop atop my miniature umbrella-like wire sculpture, enabling him to drag it out without a hitch. (See what I mean about no prayers being wasted?)

It had been a long and wearing day. Because Eliza was out of town, I decided to walk Knox one last time at 9:00 p.m. before turning in. It was not to be. She slipped her collar and, being a Beagle (for the most part), immediately proceeded to lope away into the night. My search efforts were aided by three students living nearby. Knox successfully evaded all four of us for hours. The oldest student sensed from the bandages on my neck that I ought to be in bed, so he called off the search, assuring me that the dog would find her way home.

Life is seldom easy. Having earlier driven my car several blocks away in search of Knox, I thought she might benefit from finding it back in our driveway. Walking those blocks, calling Knox, I kept praying to St. Anthony:[18] "Dear St. Anthony, come

---

18   Saint Anthony of Padua (1195–1231), commonly referred to as the finder of lost articles.

around, something's lost and can't be found." (If you're rolling your eyes, and maybe even smirking, Stop! I realize that Knox wasn't lost; she knew precisely where she was!) Upon reaching my car, I gave one last plaintive call, "Knox," whereupon she strolled up to me from across the street. I cried; had Knox; but no car—wouldn't start. Mustering my very last ounces of energy, I carried her back home. The end of a perfect day: eventful in the extreme, laced with prayers throughout, and even a happy ending.

In Gratitude

Fifteen years of fighting cancer isn't unrealistic these days. Not to say that cancer has been given a bad rap by being called a "deadly disease." Too many friends and family fallen to its diverse forms now live only as fond memories: my Uncle Joe, Mark, Welsh, Ellen, Madeline, Connie, Margie, Joni. . . . The complete list would only depress.

I've heard that some who are diagnosed with cancer react by asking, "why me?" It is only with regard to those many whose lives have been taken by the disease that I wonder: Why is it that I am still living? "Why me?"

Blessed with a brilliant, beautiful wife and three children who regularly amaze us, these added years are appreciated in the extreme. Saying "thank you" here sounds pathetically inadequate.

> "It is truly right and just, our duty and our salvation, always and everywhere to give you thanks, Lord, holy Father, almighty and eternal God, through Christ our Lord."

You may be surprised to see "cancer" on my list of reasons for giving thanks (and I'm hardly a masochist). The big reason for my being thankful may be that the chemotherapy worked! Within a year all traces of my lymphoma were gone. I experienced numbness in my hands and feet (which, counterintuitively, became hypersensitive to cold). As I learned in a cancer survivor's support group at Duquesne University, shortly after returning to teaching, the development of such post-chemotherapy "neuropathy" is fairly common. Over the course of time my life even came to include some running again, albeit at a slower pace than ever and over considerably shorter distances. Still, I had to be thankful; my Hodgkin's Disease was apparently history.

✦

Most men, as we age, become prone to developing prostate cancer. The great golfer Arnold Palmer did, and he made several public-service-announcement videos advising older guys to get their PSA (protein-specific antigen) checked. Having met

Arnold Palmer (right up there with Bishop Sheen on the charisma charts!), I followed through by taking his advice when approaching 65 years of age. "On the high side" was how a urologist vaguely assessed my PSA, and he recommended "watchful waiting." Despite his assuring me that "most men die *with* prostate cancer, but hardly anyone dies *from* it," I left his office feeling less than optimistic. Six months or so later he harvested a number of samples surgically from my prostate gland "just as a precaution." While he remained expressly confident, I wasn't. My concerns proved well founded: not only did most of the sample bits taken from my prostate prove cancerous, but the malignant cells also registered a "Gleason score" of nine (out of a possible ten). This meant they were unusually quick-developing. Since prostate cancer typically tends to be relatively slow moving, its treatment can lack that sense of urgency experienced in a war against most other forms of cancer, but not when dealing with such a high Gleason score.

That summer was filled with daily visits to Shadyside Hospital for radiation treatments, followed at summer's end by brachytherapy surgery (implanting "seeds" into the prostate to impede cancer cell growth). The surgery occurred on the Friday before Labor Day weekend, and following the procedure I had to be catheterized. Having already been back in the classroom for a week by then, I had to resume teaching on the following Tuesday, now with a bag strapped to my ankle, which proved intolerably nerve-wracking. I went straight to the hospital immediately after class to have the catheter removed after deciding that the risk of "equipment failure" was much too

Give thanks for discomfort,
don't ask for relief,
as the day will soon come
marking end to our grief.

great. (Damn the torpedoes, full speed ahead!) Fortunately, my body didn't disappoint; the semester's classes proceeded along without incident.

That all happened eleven years ago. A two-year hiatus ensued in consequence of my radiation/brachytherapy summer: two entire years without any whole-number PSA readings! Then . . . the war resumed. Chemical weapons came into play. First, a series of three injections were administered over the course of eighteen months. Then we switched to a little tablet, taken daily, which seemed to keep my PSA in check without side effects (except that I became endowed with breasts). When the tablets stopped working, we switched to 4cc—a large load—of Firmagon serum injected subcutaneously every twenty-eight days. This often produced horrific after-effects. Within another eighteen months, those injections lost their effectiveness, so they began to be supplemented with a daily quartet of Zytiga pills. (I gather that the latter drug is powerful stuff, as it has to be buffered by morning and evening doses of Prednisone.) This battle is ongoing.

Why am I thankful for cancer? There can be no question about cancer's effect upon one's outlook: the increased focus and acute awareness of how precious time is. Even so, nothing happened to me like Saul's experience of getting thrown off his horse. He became a convert on the spot; I didn't. And yet, Saul/Paul and I share a common bond: God's grace. Without doubt, God was considerably more patient with and generous to me than to Paul. Repeatedly did I spurn God's grace, only for it to be offered yet again . . . until it finally took hold in my heart.

While my drift away from God was gradual, the return leg was downright glacial. Slow in the extreme. It began on the day I was thinking (during my surreal "parasol" surgery) about how important it was for me to meet with that priest who appeared at my hospital room door, and some time thereafter when Father Shrek heard my confession in his office at St. Paul Cathedral's parish house. Not that I've been able to avoid sinning, but at least I haven't "fallen away" since then. Of course, coming back entails a great deal more than just not "falling away" again. Becoming a practicing Catholic after a long hiatus takes some work, inasmuch as Mass attendance, the Sacrament of Reconciliation, and daily prayer must all be regularized anew. This took me a long time. I'm only glad of the outcome—and very deeply appreciative of a merciful, all-forgiving God for bestowing upon me the grace to seek that result, as well as the extra time.

✦

It's how intensely one plays during *overtime* that can matter most. With reference to cancer, and surviving, perhaps "prays" ought to be substituted for "plays." While praying more these days, I continue failing to thank God often enough . . . despite the innumerable favors, grace, and mercy bestowed upon me. *Thank you, God.* (Repeat repeatedly.)

✦

My suspicion is that many of us are guilty of ingratitude toward God for the extraordinary gifts we tend to become accustomed to as part and parcel of being human. For example, we all enjoy a good laugh, but do we ever think to thank God for giving us a sense of humor?

Two courses required by my college, "Art Appreciation" and "Music Appreciation," strike me now (more than fifty-five years later!) as good examples of our thanklessness. Artists and composers naturally owe gratitude to God for the creative gifts they possess, but so too do we viewers and listeners who get to appreciate their creations! Remind me, when was the last time we gave God a standing ovation?

The more God becomes an integral part of our daily life, the more likely we'll be to express gratitude to God on a regular basis. Since I'm not there yet (despite having so very much to be thankful for), I can't help but conclude that this takes some conscious effort. We need to speak with God every day, in gratitude, lest we allow those two words to collapse, into ingratitude.

The more God becomes an integral part of our daily life, the more likely we'll express gratitude to God on a regular basis.

I'm guessing that many, if not most, of us have either written or said, "I can't thank you enough . . ." when expressing our appreciation to someone. Never is the full depth of truth in those words plumbed as when we pray them to God, yet how many of us ever have? A valuable lesson about the appropriateness of gratitude to God—beyond those myriad circumstances when we should customarily think of giving thanks—is offered by St. Thérèse of Lisieux: "often when I cry to heaven for help it is when I feel most abandoned, but then I turn to God and His saints and thank them nevertheless." God loves us all and never abandons us even when we fall, so our gratitude to God remains ever appropriate and always warranted. Let's remember to say it, pray it.

REMAINING

One of One-Hundred-Sixty-Eight

Pursuant to the first several Commandments, we are to put no false deities before God, not pray to graven images, and not take the Lord's name in vain. (An effortless yet effective habit to develop in respect of the latter Commandment is to bow your head briefly whenever saying "Jesus" or hearing his name.)

The next Commandment is that we keep holy the Sabbath Day. For many of the faithful, this amounts to attending religious services once a week. And that's about it. I'm fine with "organized religion," but many are not, and some folks pretty much abandon going to church because of that. Big mistake. Enduring traditions, religious history suggests, are more likely to develop through structured ritual. Despite that some of our Church leaders may prove to have feet of clay, don't blame God.

✦

Last night, I attended an annual dinner meeting with half a dozen fellow tax-specialist friends, several of them former students from eons ago. Besides sharing a professional interest in taxation, we're all Christians (all but one being Catholic). A member of the group told us about how she became alienated from the Catholic Church when her pastor rejected a request to baptize her recently-born child . . . supposedly, because the parishioner had, in her words, "not paid her dues" (whether in a financial sense, or because of her not regularly attending Mass and practicing her faith, was not made clear).[19]

Hearing only her part of the story, we were all offended. Of course, there's always a larger context, and we can never judge a situation unless we understand it fully. It has never been the teaching or practice of the Catholic Church to refuse to baptize a baby because the parent is too poor to put money in the collection at Mass. Therefore, I took it that there must have been another reason, such as doubt about whether she would be teaching the faith to the baby since she didn't come to Mass regularly. In any case, the take-away from this awkward situation is that it's imperative for us not to allow someone else's difficulties with the Church bump us off track.

I want to urge all pastors encountering circumstances such as this to be willing to *resolve* the perceived delinquency. In turn, congregants should not hesitate to ask what it might take to make such a problem go away. Their shared objectives ought be to get the parishioner back in church, and follow through by allowing the requested sacrament to proceed. Neither boycott nor barricade can be allowed to persist. Whereas lawyers are often heard to describe a good settlement as one in which *neither* party is satisfied, *both* parties in cases like this should pray together for a mutually satisfying solution—one that serves to restore feelings of love and respect between them.

✦

Permit me again to encourage strongly that you include a measure of formal structure in your religious observances. Follow the example that Christ gave us while on earth: he went to Synagogue on the Sabbath.

Short-circuit the middleman and pray either by yourself or with family or friends, if you absolutely must. By all means, get back with and closer to God—preferably through the church. **Do your best** to overcome the hurdle of serious disagreement with the way that your parish or its clergy reaches out pastorally. While parents often counsel their children, "just do your best," that statement is typically intended to al-

---

19   It was not explicated exactly what the nature of the parishioner's delinquency might have been. My own parish, Sacred Heart in Pittsburgh, Pennsylvania, publishes on the front page of its weekly Bulletin, certain conditions for baptism, matrimony, and parish membership (reproduced on the final page, *post*).

leviate pressures children frequently face in their academic or athletic endeavors. It's misguided because children tend to hear "do your best" as calling for them to achieve excellence! Without even pretending to lessen your obligations to God in any way, I implore you to take that entreaty as most *children* would, and **do your best to get back to church.**

If you wonder what *your best* should amount to, two indications can be gleaned from the liturgy for Sunday, February 19, 2017. In the first, the Lord orders Moses to tell the Israelites: "Be holy, for I, the Lord, your God, am holy" (Leviticus 19: 1–2). As if that were not demanding enough, the Gospel for that same day's Mass closes with, ". . . be perfect, just as your heavenly Father is perfect" (Matthew 5: 38–48). Father Joseph Santos, Jr. delivered an eloquent sermon based on those two readings during one Saturday Vigil Mass I attended at The Church of the Holy Name of Jesus, in Providence, Rhode Island. As Father Santos assured us, God doesn't demand the impossible. This is confirmed by one of the earliest Christian writings (from late in the first century), "THE DIDACHE—Teaching of the Twelve Apostles": ". . . if you are able to bear the entire yoke of the Lord, you will be perfect; but if you are not able to do this, do what you are able." We can, and are quite obviously expected to, do our *best*. This obviously requires dedication, devotion, and a long-term resolve.

Try to envision prayers on the Sabbath as the capstone of your prayerful week.

If you think your very existence is thanks to God—and isn't that what believing in God includes?—then maybe a single hour or so of worship per week is too paltry. Considering the one-hundred-sixty-eight hours that make up an entire week, it might even be considered pathetic. Try to envision your prayers on the Sabbath Day—which obviously entails attending Mass for those who are Catholic—as the capstone of your prayerful week, rather than constituting the totality of your week's worship.

✦

Pittsburgh is a *big* sports town, home to the Steelers (football), Pirates (baseball), and Penguins (hockey), among others. I've never witnessed a contest involving any of those teams that didn't last a few hours—far longer than the duration of a typical Sunday Mass. For that matter, the time involved in attending *five* weekday Masses is generally no greater than attending a *single* game! Despite my personal love of sports, it would bore me to watch a game every single day, yet I'm regularly thrilled from attending daily Mass. Open up to God, and root for your *soul* . . . to win heaven!

✦

An easy path to achieving a more prayerful life can come from harboring an increased awareness and appreciation of God's presence in our everyday surroundings. Without embracing a pantheistic belief system, can we not observe evidence of God nearly everywhere? Consider the ever-changing sky and forces of nature; contemplate the seemingly infinite variety of living species. Acknowledge them as signs of God, and you will be praying! Think about doing this. You may well find yourself smiling more, with your spirits buoyed by weaving thoughts of God into every day. Try it!

At first glance, this morning's sky (on a late-February day in Pittsburgh) appeared monochromatic grey. Then I looked again, to see: placid pools of pale dusty blue; slightly whiter and brighter highlights here and there; and all of this deployed across the heavens clad, for the most part, in the moody grey of an awakening harbor. God definitely deserved that second look, and what a rewarding benefit inured to me from not giving up too soon! Prayer is like that; the payoff comes from keeping at it.

Pray on a regular basis, habitually. Many folks these days have taken to wearing a wrist-band that serves to alert them of a need to move about or do some exercise when they've been sedentary for too long. As far as I know, there is yet to be developed a "prayer-bit" that will notify us when it's been too long since we last talked with God. (If someone reading this invents such a blessed device, am I entitled to royalties?) All of us can and ought to do better than giving God only one hour out of the one-hundred-sixty-eight hours in each week. ***Come on!***

There's Never Enough

Eliza and I moved into our present home several decades ago. Coincidentally, the move put us a few blocks closer to the residence of a friend I had met in 1968 upon first coming to Pittsburgh to accept a teaching position. Dick became my landlord, and soon thereafter our friendship developed.

Shortly after settling in, we invited Dick and his wife Susan to come over and see our new digs. At the time, Ross Perot was mounting an independent campaign to be elected President of the United States. Dick asked what I thought motivated Perot to seek the office. My response was along these lines: "Well, he certainly has enough money, more than he could possibly ever spend, and this would put his name on the pages of history."

Leaning toward me to the point of nearly falling off the hassock on which he was perched, Dick said, "You don't understand. There's never 'enough.'" Thereupon did I first become aware of how financial sharks think. Though Dick is a modest man, he is not of "modest" means, being worth many millions. His words have remained in my memory for three decades.

In fairness to Dick, I doubt that he was describing his own individual attitude toward wealth accumulation. For that matter, he may only have been speculating about what Ross Perot's attitude might be. Dick isn't a flashy fellow, but he owned his own jet plane (that he himself piloted) to make the rounds of his divers businesses, so I'm inclined to take as reliably accurate his assessment of many folks whose coffers are filled to overflowing . . . that "there's never enough" for them.

Economists refer to the "marginal utility of money," which basically means that the more of it you have, the less value yet additional money will be to you. I wouldn't know! Nevertheless do I agree completely with the "marginal utility" theory regarding accumulations of wealth.

In our material (and materialistic) world, opinions will differ toward those among us whose quest for ever-greater wealth was neatly captured by Dick's words, "there's never enough." What comes to my mind is an image attributed to something Christ said, about it being easier for a camel to pass through the eye of a needle than for a rich man to enter the Kingdom of Heaven. (As Father Stephen Palsa suggested in a

sermon, the "eye of a needle" may refer to an entry into Jerusalem that was deliberately made very narrow so that no fully loaded camel could pass through, thus maintaining the city's security against invaders.) Whenever we fall for the misbegotten
belief that more material goods will serve to ratchet-up our happiness, it's time for
a reality check. The following lyrics from a hymn composed by a pastor who lived
near Pittsburgh can serve to remind us that *temporal* possessions are only *temporary*:

> *Lord, whose then shall they be,*
> *These treasured goods we store?*
> *Shall all the wealth we gain and guard*
> *Beyond a day endure?*
>
> …
>
> *Help us to hold in trust*
> *The treasured goods we store*
> *And share them where you bid us serve*
> *The dispossessed and poor.*[20]

The last verse prays for help in sharing. The "dispossessed and poor" (alluded to
in the final line quoted above) are defenseless before the interests of a *deified market*,[21] and it may be "naïve," as Pope Francis has said, to "trust in the goodness of those
wielding economic power."

> *Hunger for power,*
> *thirst to succeed*
> *lead us away*
> *from people in need.*[22]

If we're finding "enough" (regarding wealth accumulation) to be an ever-retreat-
ing horizon, perhaps it's high time to consider defining *too much*!

---

20   Hymn, "Lord, Whose Then Shall They Be," text by Herman Stuempfle, Jr., verses 1 and 5, in *Worship*, #807.
21   Pope Francis, *Evangeli Gaudium* (On the Proclamation of the Gospel in Today's World), Chapter 2,
paragraph #56 (November 2013); *see also* Harvey, Gallagher, Fox, *The Market as God* (Cambridge, MA: Harvard
University Press, 2016).
22   Hymn, "Jesus Still Lives," by Suzanne Toolan, S.M. (b. 1927), verse 4, © 1985, World Library
Publications, Inc., in *Gather*, #302.

✦

Do you think there's an "enough" when it comes to God—a point when more *prayers* start to have marginal utility? Because our world is fraught with temptations of every imaginable sort, my sense is that, short of outright zealotry, the closer we can get to God, the better. The best we can do, to go about weaving a Kevlar-like vest impenetrable by temptation, is through prayer. Thus when it comes to prayer, to quote my friend (way out of context), "there's never enough!"

Many of us are aware of Dante's dramatic *Inferno*, tracking nine concentric circles of hell where punishments are heaped upon sins of every ilk. Similarly, in *Paradiso*, Dante traces a journey through nine spheres of heaven. Does it not seem plausible that, just as in Dante's *Paradiso*, hierarchies might actually exist in heaven?[23] Of course, I don't know whether heaven is stratified; eternal rewards could be meted-out as were the payments made to laborers in the vineyard, in Christ's parable. (All of the workers received the same bargained-for day's wage regardless of when they were hired during the day.[24]) If you are a highly competitive individual, though, perhaps it could provide an incentive for your leading a more prayerful life by imagining—and striving to attain—the highest levels heaven might offer.

✦

In these United States and a few other wealthy nations, avariciousness may be more in evidence than holiness. But bear in mind that with monetary wealth often comes ostentation or conspicuous consumption. Holiness, by contrast, tends to be modestly clothed in humility. You would not be alone by choosing a life more filled with prayer in preference to the pointless quest for excessive pecuniary accumulations. In the words of Mother Teresa, "God did not call us to be successful, but to be faithful."

---

23   Consider Matthew 5:17–19, ". . . whoever breaks one of the least of these commandments and teaches others to do so will be called least in the kingdom of heaven. But whoever obeys and teaches these commandments will be called greatest in the kingdom of heaven."
24   Matthew 20:1–16.

I'm in Love

I fear to breathe any treason against
the majesty of love,
which is the genius and god of gifts . . .

Ralph Waldo Emerson[25]

Think about love: Is there any other infinitely expandable aspect of our existence? Blessed to be the parents of three children, my wife and I love each (and every) one of them no less than do the parents of one child love her or him.

The infinite nature of God (as espoused by virtually all religions) is impossible for us to comprehend fully. We are finite; God is infinite. Love is about as close as we can get to appreciating infinity.

The complimentary close in many of my messages to Eliza or our children as well as at the conclusion of these writings (in my Acknowledgements) is "all my love." It is indeed possible to give *all* of your love to many; the love received by each is not diminished thereby.

Skeptics may argue to the contrary, perhaps along the lines that a man with two wives will not love them both equally. Be that as it may, physical love or sexually "making love" are not what I am referring to here. (Should I retreat to the Greek *agape?*) Whereas scientific studies indicate that an individual's circle of friends will top-out at approximately 150, with truly close relationships being limited to about five, the fact remains that we only have so much energy and time. Those limitations serve to explain the skeptics' arguments, without their being taken to contradict the near-infinite nature of pure love.

✦

I enjoy watching sporting events—whether "live" or on television. This is an interest not generally shared by my wife, with one very big exception: we both revel in watching our children engage in athletic pursuits. I became spellbound when watching our daughter Regina running cross country races in grammar school, and

25   "Gifts," *The Complete Essays and Other Writings of Ralph Waldo Emerson* (New York: Random House/ Modern Library, 1940), 405.

competitively rowing in an eight-woman shell in college. I also loved seeing Will, our oldest, give his all during hard-fought high school crew races and basketball games, and Brendan in lacrosse and football.

A couple of years ago, when he was living and working in Houston, Will entered the Texas Water Safari. He and a friend set out on a 261-mile nonstop canoe race. Each entry carried a radio beacon, enabling Eliza and me to track Will and David's progress through the night. We couldn't stop watching that little dot of light as it appeared to hop along the treacherous course, sometimes ahead and occasionally behind the other leading "novice" class boat. Shortly after daybreak, little more than forty-eight hours in, they finished, winning their class with the third-best time in history for a novice team. And they beat all the other "two-person aluminum canoe" entries as well. But it wasn't their success that captivated and compelled us to watch. It was love.

We've generally been spared from seeing (except in videos) our middle child, Brendan, engage in his more recent death-defying adventures: whitewater kayaking, ice climbing, and kiteboarding. It's no exaggeration to characterize them as "death defying." He not only paddles down raging rapids but also goes over waterfalls. When those waterfalls freeze, he climbs sheer cliffs of frozen ice. And he takes to the air with a surfboard beneath his feet and a giant foil tethered to his waist. GASP!

All of these moments, and a great many others like them, top my list of greatest sporting events ever. They can fill me with pride and joy. In the same vein is the admiration I feel toward my wife's writing. From our children's accomplishments in sports or classrooms, to my wife's multi-faceted writing talents, my heart's fairly bursting!

Still, the joys provided by extraordinary achievements of the four people closest to me isn't a weekly, or even monthly, event. Their celebratory accomplishments are occasional—which is often enough. Several years ago, though, a remotely analogous phenomenon set in. It occurred during my ever-deepening daily awareness of God's presence. Moments of elation began happening. This might occur while walking back to my car after attending Mass, or while walking Knox early in the morning before going to Mass, or at any random time. The Mass affords structure; the rest of these prayerful moments, albeit typically brief, involve some God-oriented focus. If pressed to identify a specific causal connection, I would probably say "prayer." Attending Mass, walking the dog, or every now and then while just going about the day, can find me either praying or just vaguely thinking about God in one way or another, whereupon it occurs: the "leap of divine joy."[26] The euphoric thrill does not always happen, but a smile is virtually guaranteed. I don't know that prayer stimulates endorphin production the way a long run can. But the elation is far greater than anything experienced during my four marathons, innumerable half marathons, and thousands of miles in training. It's strong, and make no mistake: this is a gift from God . . . a present, if you will, of God's *perceptible presence*. I can't help but think of the burning bush Moses witnessed, as recounted in Exodus 8. Although my experiences lack fire and an audible voice of God, they are nonetheless attention-grabbing and profoundly memorable. The impression is that God is signaling, "I am here," and my natural reaction/response is "Oh, my God"! As a snippet of words (taken way out of context) from a popular movie series theme song state: "I would wait in line for this / There's always room in life for this!"[27]

✦

If you do not have love in your life, you are not alive. God *is* love, and all who live in love, live in God.[28] By virtue of love's nature—there can always be more—we can approach, and occasionally even brush with, God: this is *highly* recommended!

If you do not have love in your life, you are not alive.

26   Carol Ann Smith and Eugene F. Merz, *Moment by Moment: A Retreat in Everyday Life*, Moment 12 (Notre Dame, IN: Ave Maria Press, 2000), 46.
27   Lyrics from "Extreme Ways," by Moby (2002).
28   "[I]f we love one another, God lives in us . . ." (John 4:7–19). See also, George Herbert's poem, "Love III," where God is identified as Love, in *The Oxford Book of English Verse: 1250–1900*, Arthur Quiller-Couch, ed. (1919), 286.

'Tis the Season

Because ours is a "mixed marriage" (Eliza is Presbyterian and I'm Catholic), our family will sometimes attend back-to-back religious services on Christmas Eve. Finding a church pew with space to accommodate all five of us can be tough, what with parishioners crowding into both churches' services.

I'm writing this in early December, and today is the First Friday in December of 2016. This morning's 8:30 Mass at Sacred Heart Church on Walnut Street in Shadyside—celebrated in a beautiful little side chapel—was pretty well attended. Three weeks from now, the entire main church, and maybe even that side chapel as well, will be packed full for all the Christmas Masses.

The uplifting spirit at each Christmas Mass will be palpable. Despite the stress many of those worshippers will probably have weathered in preparing for this inspirational time (home-decorating, cooking, wrapping presents, and making many other final arrangements), there'll be a nonetheless pervasive aura of joy among them. Love abounds during this sacred season.

There's a hitch: religion isn't supposed to be seasonal! Certainly not in the sense that there's intended to be some significant break, like the "off season" of a month or more with regard to most sports.

There were times, I'll confess, when religious observance seemed like a chore to me. I wasn't really involved, just going through the motions. In retrospect, it's quite clear that I had begun to drift away. Today, Christmas is of course special. So too was this morning's First Friday Mass, and yesterday morning's Mass as well. (Far from being a zealot, I'm just trying to make up for lost time.) The more my life becomes involved with God, the less I think about taking a break; I don't want one!

Religion isn't supposed to be seasonal!

✦

Two periods during the liturgical year are expressly preparatory: the season of Advent, leading up to Christmas, and the season of Lent, leading up to Easter. While both are intended to be accompanied by increased religious devotion, different moods are associated with Advent and Lent. During Advent, our anticipation builds as we count down the days to Christ's coming; a joyful mood prevails. During Lent, the mood is somber as we recall and try to emulate Christ's fasting in the desert for 40 days and 40 nights.

Many of the epistles read at Masses celebrated during Advent come from the writings of the prophet Isaiah. These make reference, for example, to the desert in bloom, and lion sleeping with the lamb—bucolic and peaceful images. It came as a surprise to me one day during this past Advent when Father Grecco, in a brief weekday Mass homily, pointed out that Isaiah was actually prophesying the resurrection of Christ at Easter!

Christmas is full of joy, but Easter is yet more glorious. Coming on the heels of 40 days of fasting and abstinence, culminating with Christ's passion and death on the cross, Easter has an almost explosive quality about it: "He is risen!" We can lose sight of this tonal difference, but that's far less likely if our devotions don't flag after Christmas. It's unfortunate that "Christmas comes but once a year," as the saying goes, yet that need not be the case; we can decide to *will* it otherwise: the Christ from Christmas is available for us every single day of every year. We should ramp-up our Advent/Christmas level of devotion during Lent in recognition that, beyond Christ's birth, what matters is his death on Good Friday and Resurrection on Easter Sunday. (Besides, as Father Grecco humorously closed one post-Christmas Sunday sermon . . . by remaining prayerful throughout the liturgical year, next Christmas will come as less of a shock to our system!)

✦

Last night, for Saturday Vigil Mass (which counts for Sunday) at Sacred Heart Church, the celebrant was Father Richard Terdine, a visiting, retired priest. I've come to appreciate his history- and art-laced sermons that always succeed in making scripture seem pertinent to the present day. You can imagine how broadly I smiled when he said, "Advent is not just about four weeks leading up to Christmas." We need to maintain that sense of preparing—the essence of Advent—all through the year.

Think about how a mother's role begins in earnest with the delivery of her child. As all know, the elation associated with a child's birth marks the Christmas season. So too should our year of prayer surge then, and continue through the year. It's actually possible to maintain that "glow" all year round!

✦

Obviously, Christmas and Easter are especially holy times for us. Beyond Christendom, however, every religion has its most sacred seasons. We all have to realize: religion should not be an on-again, off-again proposition. We can, by maintaining God's presence in our daily lives, experience a measure of the internal peace and purposeful goodness that sacred seasons inspire in us from time to time . . . and make it last year-round!

Without question, my days during those times when I was adrift were far less satisfying than my days are now. Thanks to the Lenten/Easter season, I came to recognize how far my period of drifting away had taken me, and to realize what was needed for me to recover: reconciliation, penance, and prayer. In order for you to learn from my mistakes and avoid repeating them, embrace the opportunity to integrate prayer into your being; make it a meaningful part of your very existence.

Silent Night's Sadness

Herod the Great was King of the Jews (by Roman appointment) at the time of Christ's birth. Upon hearing the Magi report a savior's birth in Bethlehem, Herod perceived a threat to his throne. He ordered the slaughter of all boys in and about the Bethlehem area who were two years of age and younger, in an effort to kill the Christ child. Heeding a message from God, Joseph fled with Jesus and Mary into Egypt, where they stayed until after Herod's death. It's easy enough for the "all is calm, all is bright" aspect of Christmas to overshadow this gruesome episode. Even today, the joyful strains of Christmas carols do not resonate with everyone—not even all Christians. For some, this can be a depressing time of the year.

It isn't irrational to experience sadness during the Christmas season—not when extreme commercialization combines with compulsory gift-giving to impose economic pressures. The hustle-bustle and bubbling-over buzz before Christmas can drain our energy. Being alone or missing loved ones in the midst of the celebratory surroundings that prevail during this time of year can likewise foster feelings of depression. Mental health professionals also refer to Seasonal Affect Disorder (SAD)—a reaction to the cold, dark days of winter—as a common cause of holiday blues.

My mother, Regina Welsh Brown, died on the day after Christmas. She was my last-surviving close relative. Perhaps I should have let my feelings show by crying more than I did. One effect that my efforts to draw closer to God have had: I shed far more tears. But rest assured, they are now tears of joy. I suspect that it's not uncommon for heightened sensitivity to accompany a more prayerful life.

Within ten days following my mother's death, I had gone through two days of "visitation" hours at Freyvogel Funeral Home, followed on the third day with Mass of Christian Burial at St. Paul Cathedral, then a flight with her casket back to New York City for burial next to my father's grave in St. Mary's Cemetery on Staten Island: *Tristeza*! Now I was back home in Pittsburgh, trying to catch my breath, but it was early January, and I had to get ready for teaching my spring-semester classes.

A light dusting of snow greeted me on the morning of the semester's first class. It wasn't enough to cause risky road conditions, or pose any real problem, but the cold of wind-chill bit my face during the bicycle ride down Beeler Street on the way to school. With eyes watering enough behind my glasses to compromise vision, I became wary of parked cars on my right and commuter traffic passing on the left. An awareness of being alone came over me: What if I wipe out and get killed doing this? Who would claim the body? Where would they bury me?

All the willows bow in weeping.
All the rivers rage and mean.
As creation joins our pleading:
"God, do not leave us alone."[29]

I couldn't help associating Christmas with my mother's death for years thereafter. As Christmas approached, the same gray cloud would always roll in. I demurred to questions concerning my desired Christmas presents, knowing they could not fill the void but only reinforce its presence. During that time and in the subsequent years, I tried to hide my sadness from others. While not exactly "laughing on the outside," I sure was "crying on the inside." Only recently did I become aware that this had been a period of *spiritual desolation* for me; it's when my drift away from God and church set in. As Sister Carole Riley astutely observed, my mother's death was for me akin to when a youngster who has learned to ride a bicycle first attempts to do so without training wheels. Since the strongest spiritual influence had always been my mother, this analogy is extraordinarily apt.

✦

St. Paul Cathedral had a great many worshipers attending noon Mass today, the Tuesday leading up to Palm Sunday. Father Stubna's sermon repeatedly cautioned us against "spiritual amnesia" (an expression I had never heard before). It occurred to me that during the months and years while I was away from the church and no longer praying, those words accurately captured my condition. I didn't deal with my amnesia at all well. At some point after my mother died, I forgot about my Catholic upbringing, stopped thinking about and talking with God, and simply drifted away. You can do better by observing, learning from, and avoiding my mistakes.

---

29   Hymn, "Once We Sang and Danced with Gladness," by Susan Briehl, verse 2, in *Worship*, #477.

A good tactic could have been for me to engage more with friends and make gifts . . . acts of kindness, or favors, in preference to wrapped-up presents. While it's not uncommon to engage in "retail therapy"—making purchases as a means of feeling better—there's truth in the old adage, "it's better to give than to receive." Generosity to others might not be the first thing that comes to mind when you're sad at Christmas or any other time (after all, you're feeling sorry for yourself!), but this is a good cure, certainly worth trying.

The following prayer from the Book of Esther could also have helped:

Save us by your hand, and help me, who am alone and have no helper but you, O Lord. O God almighty, hear the voice of the despairing, save us from the hands of evildoers, and save me from my fear. (Esther 12: 23–25)

✦

I ought to have known better than to feel so alone, based on what had happened at the funeral home when my mother was there. She had become severely hearing impaired with age, but obtained help from a non-profit agency: Pittsburgh Hearing, Speech, and Deaf Services (PHSDS—now the Center for Hearing and Deaf Services, or HDS). During the first afternoon at Freyvogel's, many HDS employees showed up, led by Executive Director Marlene Roberts together with the agency's audiologist, Alison Weber. I had never met any of them before, yet they all came. This was such a collective outpouring of sympathy that it bowled me over. (I've actively worked with HDS ever since.)

Just as the second afternoon's visitation hours ended, in walked Harry Gruner, a graduate of Pitt Law School and long-time fellow "car nut" friend. He spirited me away to the North Hills, where his wife Chris was making dinner for us at their home. She even baked a big batch of chocolate-chip cookies for afterwards! Two hours later, I hastened from his Porsche 911 into Freyvogel's for the final two hours of visitation, feeling whole again. When the darkest of times are met with love like this, how can we possibly overlook God? The notion of God as *love* is inviting indeed! As the final line in the opera "Hansel and Gretel" says, "When past bearing is our grief / Then it is that God the Father sends relief."

Congregate!

No matter what your religion, great strength can be derived from attending services in the same house of worship on a regular basis. Faces of other attendees will start to become familiar, and friendships will gradually develop. Some religious communities are definitely more sociable than others, but try to get to know your priest, and at least some of your fellow parishioners.

"Shop" for a parish with whose members you feel comfortable and to whom you can relate, if you wish. Or search out a priest whose messages in sermons tend to resonate with you. Join a faith community, attend "religiously," and get closer to God. Gathering with other good people in prayer should serve to reinforce the religious practices of all in the group. Take heed the benefits of congregating, as Jesus described them: "I say to you, if two of you agree on earth about anything for which they are to pray, it shall be granted to them by my heavenly Father. For where two or three are gathered together in my name, there am I in the midst of them" (Matthew 18:15-20).

Upon first formally joining Sacred Heart Parish in Pittsburgh, I prepared a very brief bio to introduce myself. It never saw the light of day. Despite having tried hard not to toot my own horn, concern remained that my mini-bio might sound braggadocio. A couple of years later, when I began to consider the idea of possibly studying to become a deacon, it became necessary to compose something along the same lines. Then, my pastor related how useful it was for him to have such information in order to become familiar with his parishioners: "Only with knowledge of your background and skillsets can we know when it's appropriate for us to consider calling upon you," Father Grecco told me. He now knows more about me (including that my age disqualifies me from becoming a deacon!).

Remember, you're not applying for employment, or even for a non-paying volunteer position, with the basic bio you humbly hand to the head of your congregation. It should be on the modest side. Short and sweet, but not sugar-coated. The objective, obviously, is for you to become involved. Involvement at any level, in virtually any way, stands in sharp contrast to indifference. (You already know how I feel about indifference!)

My highly abbreviated autobiography did its job. After an impressively thorough background check was conducted, I obtained clearance to serve as a Lector at Sacred Heart Church. This entails my reading of the Epistle aloud, from the altar, during weekday Mass (not having yet developed sufficient stage presence to do so in front of a crowded church on Sundays!). Following the Epistle, the congregation is led through a "Responsorial Psalm." Those in attendance say their response aloud, repeatedly, while I go through a short litany of brief (generally one- or two-sentence-long) prayers. It's all simple enough, but doing this greatly enriches the Mass-attending experience for me—as it could for you as well.

As a Lector, you will want to arrive early for Mass and gain some familiarity with the readings. At Sacred Heart parish church, Father Grecco always has the book placed on a lectern, already opened to that day's readings. Whoever is going to read aloud during the Mass studies the relevant passages to get their gist, works out the pronunciation of any unfamiliar individual or place names, and tries to anticipate where pause-points and emphases will best occur during the oral reading. By virtue of doing these brief preparations, the readings become *your own* and their message resonates with you. I love participating in the Mass as a Lector; it magnifies the experience of attending Mass to the point that even on days when I'm not reading, more is gained from just being there.

Don't hesitate to become involved out of concern that it could prove burdensome. You'll most likely feel more connected with your church, as well as with God. This enhanced level of engagement is truly enjoyable.

For me, Sacred Heart Church in Pittsburgh feels like home. It's where all three of our children were baptized—notwithstanding that I remained "fallen away" during the time. Despite my allegiance to this parish, there will occasionally be a more conveniently scheduled Mass at St. Paul Cathedral, or St. Bede, that I'll attend. (We never want "the best" to become enemy of "the good," and it's always good to attend Mass—even daily, if possible.) Whenever traveling, check masstimes.org to locate the nearest church(es) to your destination and the times when Masses are celebrated there. Pick your target, and always attend Mass, at very least on Sundays (or Saturday Vigil Mass) and holy days.

We missed out in one instance, though, when as a many-hours-long drive to Providence, Rhode Island ended, it turned out the Mass I'd selected from MassTimes wasn't being said! On other occasions there have been anxious moments while trying to find the chosen church in time; we use Eliza's cell phone for navigation, but when heavy traffic combines with unfamiliar city surroundings, confusion can readily result. Someone suggested that we might fare better by driving a Kia "Soul" model because they're supposedly equipped with a highly accurate GPS—Global Positioning System. (Otherwise, I suppose, many a Soul might be lost!) As Saint Paul once wrote, in a completely different context, ". . . put up with a little foolishness from me! Please put up with me" (2 Corinthians 11:1–2).

S U S T A I N I N G

Matthew's Gospel, written during the first century after Christ's Resurrection, aimed at Jews as the then most likely prospective converts. The parable Christ told about sown seeds[30] had particular pertinence to Jews, and included a whimsical twist: Water was scarce in the area of Jerusalem, yet seed was even more precious, making the indiscriminate sowing in this parable seem nearly ridiculous. Some of the sown seeds fell on the path, to be eaten by birds; some fell upon rocky soil, and although they germinated, the thin soil would not support sufficient rooting for plants to survive; and some fell among thorns that choked-out the young seedlings; but some landed in rich soil, sprouted, and returned many-fold.[31] Because Christ didn't square with many Jews' expectations concerning the Messiah, some of them by analogy fell into the first three groups of ill-fated seeds, as do some Christians; we must enrich our souls to offer fertile ground for God's words to thrive. That's what this "Sustaining" segment is about.

---

30 Matthew 13:1–23 (USCCB).

31 As Jesus explained, "The seed is the word of God. Those on the path are the ones who have heard, but the Devil comes and takes away the word from their hearts that they may not believe and be saved. Those on rocky ground are the ones who, when they hear, receive the word with joy, but they have no root; they believe only for a time and fall away in time of temptation. As for the seed that fell among thorns, they are the ones who have heard, but as they go along, they are choked by the anxieties and riches and pleasures of life, and they fail to produce mature fruit. But as for the seed that fell on rich soil, they are the ones who, when they have heard the word, embrace it with a generous and good heart, and bear fruit through perseverance" (Luke 8:4–15).

Spelled Backwards

It concerns me that many folks might not come naturally to *deeply love God*. We say prayers for thanksgiving and prayers of petition, which are altogether good, of course; they indicate that we believe in, trust, and embrace God. All the same, those "three little words" belong in the mix.[32] When lifting our hearts and minds to God (which is the way grade-school catechisms traditionally define "prayer"), let's include "I love you." To many of us, this may not feel natural at first because our notion of Almighty God can tend to get in the way. Perhaps we need to *befriend* God, before it's possible for God to become *beloved* by us.

Think about how wonderful it would be to live during Christ's time on earth, know this God-made-man, and count him as your own personal friend! Wait . . . we still can! He's with us now as much as then, and just as available for us to love deeply.

For us to love God as much as we are loved by God is impossible. While our finite capabilities are no match for God's infinite nature, we can nonetheless reach out . . . and sing "Christo Yo Te Amo."[33]

✦

Loving God *deeply* requires that we move beyond the conceptualizing of our creator as an abstraction.[34] Jesus Christ, who walked on this earth as a man, affords us the obvious means of doing so. His very presence on earth was the greatest gift given to mankind—but then it was magnified beyond mere mortals' imagination by his dying for us on the cross. Christ's life and death were hardly abstractions.

✦

A snippet of lyrics in a hymn I vaguely remember from eons ago refers to God as the "bridegroom of my soul." Those words were learned by all of us preparing to receive our "First Holy Communion" (the Blessed Sacrament of the Eucharist) some sixty-five years ago. Perhaps the "bridegroom" reference is why "Please, marry me"

---

32   See, e.g., "I love you, O Lord," Psalm 18:2–3a.

33   Spanish worship song, "Jesus I Love You."

34   Saint Maria Faustina Kowalska, in *Diary: Divine Mercy in My Soul* (Stockbridge, MA: Marian Press, 2008), 511, recounts what she believes Jesus told her about the indifference of souls toward him, and their distrust of him: "They treat me as a dead object."

are the words that will occasionally initiate my moments of prayer. Any "marry me" message cannot help but include "I love you," but it's the emotional attachment underlying those words that we need.[35]

✦

While on the way to our woodland retreat house (*Trifol*) two weeks ago, with Knox in my lap and Eliza driving, I asked her whether she thought most folks loved God, or their dog, more. After thinking about this, her answer came, haltingly, "the dog." I agreed. And last weekend, when we asked our son Will's godmother, Cathy Kelly, she gave us the same answer.

It's important to realize that my objective wasn't to craft an accusatory situation by posing this question. I had suspected that, at least when first asked, many dog lovers (myself included) would sheepishly (if not doggedly) admit to loving their dogs to a greater extent . . . at least if they were being honest. Let's think about that.

We were having dinner several weeks ago with Larry Leventon, who long ago was a student in the first course I taught at the University of Pittsburgh. While telling us about a friend of his whose dog had recently died, Larry quoted the friend as saying, "It's just like losing a child."

The moment I heard Larry say this, my mind clouded over with dark thoughts. Several decades ago, Larry lost a son shortly after the child was born. I remember when this happened, and recall Larry telling me about riding with his infant son in the back of an ambulance on a long, harrowing trip to the finest medical facility available. When Larry's son died, the pain he suffered back then was now replaying across his face as he conversed with us over dinner. His grief was manifestly greater than ever could have been experienced as a result of the death of a beloved dog. Without mincing words, Larry had told his grieving friend, whose dog recently died, "It's not the same [as losing a child]."

✦

God the Father sent *his only begotten Son* to die, by serving as our savior on the cross. Is it not clear that *we ought to love God more than we do our dog*? If we know

---

35   *See, e.g.,* "Behold, the Bridegroom is coming; come out to see Christ the Lord" (Matthew 25:6).

that we should, what's stopping us? The wagging tail, the greeting when we arrive home, the soft fur and submissive eyes? Those and other adorable aspects of dogs get to us every time, I realize. While I would never ask anyone, "love your dog less," I can't help but suggest that we love God *more*.

Christians believe that Christ came to earth and gave up his life for us some two thousand years ago. The son of God became man in order to serve as our savior. He did so in fulfillment of prophesy and scripture. Repeatedly did Christ assure that he was The One. With numerous miracles he affirmed this truth. God-made-man died for you, for me, for each and every one of us. Do we not *love* God for making that sacrifice? Love God *deeply* for doing so? Without a doubt, we should.

✦

Let's turn the tables. Do you actually think that your dog could love you more than God does? Is it not obvious that anyone answering that query in the affirmative would be barking up the wrong tree? We owe our very existence to God! It was God's Son, Jesus Christ, who re-opened the gates of heaven to us. It was the Father's Son who died for us! What has your dog done? In the overall scheme of things, isn't it evident that God loves us more?[36] Perhaps you never thought about this before. Now that you have, it's appropriate to consider whether you love God *deeply*.

From now on, when you interact with your dog or other pet, consider thinking about God as well. That way, your pet can serve as a friendly reminder of God! The reason we love dogs so much is because they're such loving creatures; we naturally tend to reciprocate by loving them back. God loves us too, even more than does any dog or other pet, and we ought reciprocate accordingly.

✦

Not long after Christ's Resurrection, he commissioned the apostles to go forth and teach all nations. Local authorities forbid them from doing so, but they persisted—at times flagrantly, in front of the synagogue. These holy men recognized their

---

36   Heed the assurance in Isaiah (49:12–15) that God's love is even greater than that of a mother towards her child: "Can a mother forget her infant, be without tenderness for the child of her womb? Even should she forget, I will never forget." And in St. Paul's letter to the Ephesians (3:14–19): "Know the love of Christ that surpasses knowledge."

allegiance to God over those who sought to silence them. Often, in our own lives, do we face an analogous choice between temporal and spiritual matters. While dogs are creatures of God—perhaps even gifts from God—I regard them as pertaining to this world, to this life, rather than the next. Wouldn't you agree?

God begins loving you at the instant of your conception and never stops loving you, even when you stumble or fall.

Anyone who's a dog-lover, animal-lover, or nature-lover is primed and ready to love God. (Perhaps they already do, whether or not consciously.) An *intimate* relationship with God thrives on love. God begins loving you at the instant of your conception and never stops loving you, even when you stumble or fall.

The prodigal son story should convince us of God's unflagging love, as does the shepherd's joy from finding a lost lamb. Due to our human frailties, most of us can envision ourselves in the role of prodigal son or lost lamb. By considering how joyous are the prodigal son's father and the shepherd (both of whom represent God in those parables) when whoever "once was lost but now [is] found,"[37] we can appreciate just how merciful, forgiving, and loving God is. Only by *deeply loving* God will our appreciation best be manifest.

God's love embraces me
God's love envelops me
. . . completely
God's love maintains me
God's love sustains all of us,
minute by minute.
God is Love, for eternity.

If we love God and try our very best not to compromise that love by any antithetical actions (or inaction), there's no need to be distracted by thoughts about when the music might stop. Keep in mind that *God deserves all our love*, every day of our lives. Thanks to the fact that Jesus Christ was given to us by the Father, became man, and actually walked on earth, "God" isn't an abstract concept with which our minds must struggle to cope.[38] Neither is God par-

---

37   Lyrics from "Amazing Grace," Gospel Song, John Newton, 1725–1807.

38   "The Incarnation of the Son of God has given sight to us men who were groping in darkness; He who dwelt among us has thrown a light on the Divine Nature which does not shine from the ablest treatise on philosophy." The Most Rev. M. Sheehan, DD, *Apologetics and Catholic Doctrine* (Dublin: M. H. Gill & Son, 1937); revised by F. Peter Joseph (London: St. Austin, 2000).

ticularly challenging for our hearts to embrace with love. The Son of God suffered excruciating agony and ultimately died *for us*. It should be easy for us to love God back, *deeply*.

In our personal relationships, the better we get to know someone, the more we can come to like and eventually love them. It's no different with God: to know is to love. We just need to open our eyes, minds, and hearts to God by living loving, prayerful lives.

Habits to Develop

We're all human. For most of us, that means mistakes will be made. Our proclivity to err demands that we persevere: keep trying. Rather than falling prey to feelings of hopelessness, always **Persevere**.

An insightful analysis of the point of view that can lay waste to *perseverance*, by fostering discouragement or despair, is offered by St. Thérèse of Lisieux (1874–1897): "When we yield to discouragement or despair, it is usually because we give too much thought to the past and to the future."[39]

✦

I know, there are times . . . and yet, provoking pity from those who love us isn't particularly refreshing. Those individuals who thrive most admirably don't let defeat extinguish their efforts. They exhibit an indomitable spirit, never running out of hope. Let the notion that "hope springs eternal" fuel you. Always **Maintain Hope**.

The opposite of *hope* is *despair*. In order to maintain **hope** in our lives, we must continually resist despair. *Despair*, as described by Thomas Merton, "is the ultimate development of a pride so great and stiff-necked that it selects the absolute misery of damnation rather than accept happiness from the hands of God and thereby acknowledge that [God] is above us and that we are not capable of fulfilling our destiny by ourselves." Based on Merton, can you discern/explain how prayer helps maintain hope?

✦

It may seem strange, but mistakes and failures can sometimes prove easier to weather than our successes. That's because humility will often be difficult to come by in those happy circumstances when we succeed. There's a biblical story about two men who visit the synagogue. One of them, who thinks quite highly of himself, proceeds up close to the altar and basically boasts to God about his accomplishments. The other man remains at the rear of the synagogue; he prays there simply because he feels unworthy; and he begs for God's mercy. As if you didn't know, it's the hum-

---

39   Vernon Johnson, *Spiritual Childhood: The Spirituality of St. Thérèse of Lisieux* (San Francisco: Ignatius Press, 2001), 121.

ble one who sets a better example. As Pope Francis recently observed, "The more powerful you are, the more your actions will have an impact on people, the more responsible you are to act humbly."[40] *Be Humble.*

✦

Just before serving the Holy Eucharist to communicants, the priest elevates the chalice together with a consecrated host and says, "Behold the Lamb of God, behold Him who takes away the sins of the world. Blessed are those called to the supper of the Lamb." In reply, the faithful express their humility while seeking God's forgiveness with: "Lord, I am not worthy that you should enter under my roof, but only say the word and my soul will be healed."[41] With the second phrase, we see "my roof" become a metaphor—now meaning our own soulful body. It is at this juncture that communicants approach the altar and receive the Holy Eucharist. Behold: God is with us *and* we are with God! *Keep Acknowledging God's Presence At All Times.*

✦

So many of us fall down in our faith repeatedly, committing basically the same sins over and over. It's discouraging. We can even become embarrassed enough about our "repeat offender" status to stop going to confession. (Been there, done that.) Securing forgiveness for our sins requires sincere repentance and penance coupled with a resolve to sin no more. Fortunately, God's patience leaves the door open for us to seek forgiveness, but we have to trust in God's mercy. When Christ prayed for those who tortured and eventually killed him, by saying "Forgive them, Father, for they know not what they do," he offered us an insight into the depths of Godly Mercy. If only we can keep believing in God's infinite love and mercy, it will remain within our grasp to have a seat in heaven when the music stops. *Keep Believing and Trusting in God.*

✦

40   TED 2017, "The Future You" (April 2017), www.ted.com/talks/pope-francis-why-the-only-future-worth-building-includes-everyone?language=en.
41   The first phrase in that passage parallels what the centurion said when the soldier sought-out Christ to cure his servant, who was seriously ill. Basically, the centurion suggested that Jesus perform this miracle without actually entering the house—and that is what Jesus did.

The most memorable line in Erich Segal's bestseller, *Love Story*, is "Love means never having to say you're sorry." Those words can be parsed in differing ways. First, one's love is so strong and pure in commitment that there'll never be any occasion that warrants an apology. This first take poses an ideal objective in our relationship with God: never to sin. After all, God is the one we love, the one we shouldn't hurt at all.

The second variation suggests that someone who's truly loved knows with confidence that the person who loves them would never deliberately cause any pain. Therefore, an apology can be presumed without need for its articulation in the event something hurtful happens to occur. This might sound like an agreeable enough alternative at first, but it actually presents an unacceptably poor choice.

Any thoughts, words, or actions (as well as inaction) not in keeping with God's plan for us should provoke an immediate "I'm sorry" to God. Loving God means *always* having to say you're sorry!

By dissecting Erich Segal's *Love Story* line, we can perceive reasons why one might fail to avail of the Sacrament of Reconciliation. Although these are polar opposite situations, it's actually possible for us to alternate between them. (The devil is indeed a clever foe!) Fortunately, a readily available solution for both is to go to confession regularly! Confess everything that an earnest examination of conscience enables you to recall. Don't let "small stuff" ride, or you'll start to drift.

Assuming we love God with all our mind, heart, and strength, it is nonetheless fitting and right to confess any misstep, even if but a venial (rather than mortal) sin. We all have our weaknesses; the trick is to keep them under control—without allowing anything more serious to develop. ***Always Confess All (even minor) Sins!***

✦

You will doubtless understand why I never want to draw an analogy to cancer, but it's too apt not to do so here. Relatively minor transgressions, if left unchecked (i.e., unconfessed), can all too readily metastasize into a bigger problem. Best we recognize our failings while they remain small, and expiate them through the Sacrament of Reconciliation. Like cancer, sin can kill us if we don't catch it early enough. Savor this solace: it's considerably easier to confess a venial sin than a mortal sin (at least, that's been my experience). Thus, by taking early action, our lives get easier, and better: it's such a good deal!

The best approach for keeping our sins to a minimum, in both quantity and seriousness, is through regular confession. I've witnessed the Sacrament of Reconciliation fall from favor during my adult life: there used to be long lines of penitents; a good Catholic would tend to go to confession every other week, if not weekly. Why has this changed? Some folks may have become more casual about morality. (The evil one is no doubt overjoyed by our *failure to notice* when we're not living this life as God intends.) More regular confession could cure that, and because it feels so good to confess, it's foolish not to. Other individuals might shy away from confession due to their guilt feelings. While that probably sounds ironic, it can happen (been there . . .). We become so self-absorbed with our own sense of sinfulness that God's infinite mercy and forgiving nature are forgotten. Anyone tied up in that pretzel-knot needs to contemplate George Herbert's "Love" poem:

> *Love bade me welcome; yet my soul drew back,*
> > *Guilty of dust and sin.*
> *But quick-eyed Love, observing me grow slack*
> > *From my first entrance in,*
> *Drew nearer to me, sweetly questioning*
> > *If I lack'd anything.*
>
> *'A guest,' I answer'd, 'worthy to be here:'*
> > *Love said, 'You shall be he.'*
> *'I, the unkind, ungrateful? Ah, my dear,*
> > *I cannot look on Thee.'*
> *Love took my hand and smiling did reply,*
> > *'Who made the eyes but I?'*[42]

42   George Herbert, "Love III," from *The Temple: Sacred Poems and Private Ejaculations* (Cambridge: 1633), reproduced in Arthur Quiller-Couch, ed., *The Oxford Book of English Verse: 1250–1900* (1919), 286; see also, *George Herbert and the Seventeenth-Century Religious Poets*, ed. Mario A. Di Cesare (New York: W. W. Norton, 1978), 69.

From just these two verses, it should be obvious that Love is God, and we (you, or I) are the reluctant and humble guest—professing ourselves to be unworthy of being in Love's presence. Yet God accepts us, with a smile. Consider taking this poem with you to receive the Sacrament of Reconciliation, bearing in mind why you're there: **Always Accept God's Infinite Love, Mercy, and Forgiveness**.

During yesterday's Vigil Mass (September 30, 2017), Father Foriska's homily included the story of a penitent who had difficulty accepting God's forgiveness for her sins. Her priest instructed her to seek God's help, specifically by asking God to tell her what sin the priest had committed while in the seminary. When she next came to confession, her priest inquired whether this had been done. "Yes," she replied, "and God came to me in a dream, with the answer." "What did God tell you?" the priest asked. "God told me he forgot." While we may not be so able to forget grievances against us, God not only forgives but also forgets! **Accept That God Forgives and Forgets Our Sins!**

✦

Forty days after Christ was born (from December 25th to February 2nd on our calendar), Mary and Joseph complied with holy law by presenting their baby boy in the temple. Two individuals of special note were there in the temple at that time. One was Simeon, an elder who was promised by the Holy Spirit that he would not die before seeing the Messiah. Simeon had long awaited this day; he was well aware of who Christ was when Mary and Joseph brought the infant into the temple, and he predicted that Jesus would grow up to become "a light to the Gentiles, the Glory of Israel." Also present was Anna, a prophetess who had been in the temple for a very long time, praying and fasting day and night. She was eighty-four years old when the Christ child was presented. We're probably all aware that "patience is a virtue," but how many of us emulate the patience of Simeon and Anna? If we want to see God, patience is absolutely necessary; "be prepared to endure everything with patience . . ." (Colossians 1:12).

I have a history of being impatient: as an only child, I was accustomed to getting my way when growing up; and as an adult, my irritability persisted. It remains a problem, though I keep trying to overcome my weakness. Is this a big deal? Unfortunately, yes, it is. Impatience tends to beget anger; it can easily lead to loss of temper.

Notice what's happening here: love is dying! We absolutely need to maintain our love of God. That's obvious. In turn, we must interact with our fellow man in a similar way by not becoming impatient, getting angry, or losing control. Since one of the Commandments forbids anger, hatred, revenge . . . we're drifting into mortal sin territory . . . and no longer hearing the music, which could stop unexpectedly at any moment. Even when impatience doesn't involve "blowing your top," it's at least a venial sin. Confess it! It's when we "don't sweat the small stuff" as sinners that we drift away . . . as I know all too well. Don't let that happen to you. ***Be Patient!***

✦

Over the course of nearly fifty years, I've been either a runner of sorts or a "sort of" runner—which is to say most of the time casual, but occasionally somewhat serious. (It's hardly a religious activity: only very rarely will I "see" God during a run; more often, a few prayers might be said—just to keep me going.) As I know all too well, injuries or illness can quickly reverse the usually beneficial effects—increased endurance and greater speed—that gradually result from regular training. I've had a fair number of setbacks that rendered me slower, over ever-shorter distances. Even so, I went along when my good friend Don Sutton, a superior runner who thinks that at our age the half-marathon is equivalent to a marathon, proposed that we enter the Buffalo Creek Half. It's a low-key, relatively straight-line race, run on a scenic, predominantly flat course in mid-October. As race day approached, the 13.1-mile distance loomed long and downright daunting to me. I visited St. Paul Cathedral and very slowly walked, contemplatively, through the Stations of the Cross. Thinking about Jesus's extraordinary suffering during those last hours, concentrating on Christ's agony, led me to conclude: "What's in store for me is chicken-feed compared with this." Don medaled, and I finished! ***Never Overlook an Occasion for Prayer, or Underestimate its Power!***

Agony of Gethsemane
and pathos from "Pieta,"
Spare me not such pain, Oh Lord—
Share them with me still—
As I wend my way toward you,
Striving to do your Will.

No Alibis or Excuses

Because all of us are human, we're prone to sin. (I won't define *sin*, since everyone with a conscience should know what I mean.)[43]

At the same time, we want to feel good about ourselves. There is a natural tendency, therefore, to cast a blind eye toward our sins. We naturally don't want to look into that mirror, lest we see our faults; so, instead, we tend to look away. And we may even attempt to becloud the reflection of our wrongs by making up alibis, excuses, rationalizations, or explanations. While these techniques might serve to assuage our guilt to some extent, they offer no more than symptomatic relief. Please don't avail of those pain relievers! Whereas feeling guilty is uncomfortable, the discomfort of guilt can actually prove desirable as an incentive for going to confession.

There is a natural tendency to cast a blind eye toward our sins.

Whenever we have had the nerve to *offend God*, it becomes incumbent upon us to muster the courage to admit to ourselves that *we messed up!* There is a profound need for us to face our faults: Admit them first to yourself and then in the Sacrament of Reconciliation. Otherwise, by failing to acknowledge the sins we commit, we become ever more likely to repeat them and fail to repent for them. Forgiveness is a shining light that beckons to us from the end of that dark tunnel our sins put us in. We can walk out!

But we will remain trapped in the tunnel of darkness if we rationalize, explain-away, excuse, or develop alibis for our sin(s). While those circuit-breakers might work to stop your conscience from bothering you, the stain of sin will still remain. Why not wipe away your guilt and the regret of having done wrong? All it takes is simply to seek forgiveness from God. Whenever we are genuinely contrite and resolve to get back on the straight and narrow, our all-merciful God grants absolution! God's gift of

---

43   *See* Claire Gecewicz, "Most U.S. Catholics Rely Heavily on Their Own Conscience for Moral Guidance," April 19, 2016, www.pewresearch.org/fact-tank/2016/04/19/most-catholics-rely-on-their-own-conscience-for-moral-guidance. Lest any reader be unable to continue without some definition of *sin*, it's "an obstacle that prevents us from being our best selves." Macrina Diederkehr, *Seven Sacred Pauses* (Notre Dame, IN: Sorin, 2008), 159.

forgiveness is being offered to all of us; we just have to accept it—by being a penitent. Why in heaven's name would anyone ever want to pass that up?!

✦

I trust that, by my disparaging common "explanations" we might conjure in order to cover-over wrongdoing, readers will not be led to peruse the Bible in the manner comedian W.C. Fields once claimed he was doing, with the purpose of "looking for loopholes"!

Temptation

Eliza and I met Will at a local bakery this morning, where he suggested that I try the chocolate almond croissant. I took his advice. The pastry was pretty good, but so overloaded with cream filling that it was not worth the calories. Since I'd like to lose weight, I especially regretted consuming it. "You just need to forego something else that would be bad for you," Will kidded me. The problem is that not all temptations are equivalent; some are definitely more difficult to resist than others. I should have passed up eating the croissant, but didn't.

We need to be aware and mindful of the fact that certain circumstances will tend to lead us into committing sin. A clear correlation will be there, whether place-related, people-related, or both; this includes some websites and search-engines. For good reason, these "proximate occasions of sin" absolutely *must* be avoided. (Metaphorically speaking, the bakery this morning was a proximate occasion for stuffing my face with that chocolate almond croissant!)

W e need to be aware and mindful of the fact that certain circumstances will tend to lead us into committing sin.

We all have our weak spots. That explains why we find ourselves having to confess the same sins over and over. What to do? In footnote number 3, I suggested developing a *trigger* that would lead to praying a Hail Mary whenever impure thoughts begin to form. At least for me, under those circumstances, a prayer to Mary has proved effective at nipping those thoughts in the bud. Invoking the Blessed Mother on such occasions tends to make me feel embarrassed! Let's go to school on that technique, and explore whether it might have other applications.

First we have to identify our weak spot(s): Is there anything offensive to God, that you find yourself doing repeatedly—or something pleasing to God, that you regularly omit or even simply forget to do? Do you *ever* foresee that offensive behavior or omission looming on the horizon? Take note of any such "early warning signs." They can serve as the basis for developing your awareness of when the wheels are beginning to get wobbly—before they fall off! That awareness, in turn, can be crafted into a "prayer trigger." Once operative, the *trigger* should provoke you to say a well-select-ed prayer: one that proves effective at either dissuading you from committing your weak-spot sin or persuading you to engage with God. (In this regard, do not overlook the power of invoking the name of Jesus.)

Admittedly, this entire process is considerably easier for me to write about than it is for either of us to put into actual practice. Even so, with determination, perse-verance, and prayer, it could work . . . and it's well worth the effort to eliminate our "repeat offender" status!

✦

It's mid-February (2017), and every day during this week the Epistles are from Genesis . . . starting this past Monday with "let there be light" (concerning the first four days of creation) and progressing to today, Friday, addressing the serpent's lies that tricked Eve and Adam. I served as Lector and spoke the devil's words[44] with treachery in my tone. (A stranger stopped me as I was leaving church, to say how much she had enjoyed the sinister way in which I voiced the serpent; my only hope is that the devil really hated it!)

No one needs me to tell them there's evil in this world. (I just wish no one needed to be persuaded that there's a God.) As today's Epistle demonstrates, however, we all need to remember: we *will* be subjected to temptations, repeatedly and regularly, without any warning. The critically important first step in *resisting* temptation is *rec-ognizing* it. And, in the immortal words of Mortimer Snerd (voiced by ventriloquist Edgar Bergan), "It ain't easy."

There *is* another team; the serpent in today's Epistle was on that other team, but didn't disclose that fact to Eve. The evil one never admits to being an enemy, or mem-ber of the "other team"; we have to pick up on that despite the devil's many disguises.

During the late stages of writing this little book, I allowed myself the luxury of sporadically reading *This Side of Paradise*, F. Scott Fitzgerald's first novel, while being

---

44   From Genesis 3:1–8, The serpent said to the woman (who we call Eve), after she had recounted to him God's admonition against even touching, let alone eating, fruit from the tree in the middle of the garden, lest she die: "You certainly will not die! No, God knows well that the moment you eat of it your eyes will be opened and you will be like gods who know what is good and what is evil." What conniving duplicity this was, and, sadly, it worked. Lessons to be learned: don't underestimate the evil enemy; be vigilant; be on guard; be on God!

amused by thoughts that my focus was on *the other* side of paradise. As fate would have it (God's fingerprints?), Monsignor Thayer Darcy writes a letter to Fitzgerald's chief protagonist, Amory Blaine, about ". . . that half-miraculous sixth sense by which you detect evil, it's the half-realized fear of God in your heart." Who am I to take issue with a Monsignor—even a fictitious one? We need to fine-tune our Satan-seeing radar—and whenever thus alerted become like Christ: as man, Jesus was subjected to temptation and reacted sternly by saying, "begone, Satan"!

Realize that with the "other team" it's always recruiting season; and bear in mind that no NCAA rules limit the perks that team promises in order to get you signed up. Worse yet, they're always false promises. The devil lies—what a surprise—and you can rely on that! It just so happens that I'm in New England while writing this. Folks hereabouts are not infrequently heard to use the word *wicked* with reference to any number of things, both good and bad! Make no mistake about the fact that the "other team" is wicked in only one sense—the bad, evil sense of *wicked*, bereft of any admirable qualities. Don't fall for the snazzy uniform or signing bonus they may offer you: *Via con Dios* (Go with God)!

We are always subjected to temptations, repeatedly and regularly, without warning.

I'll lay it out for you: God is good, and a life lived close to God can be downright great, ever improving the closer we get. But the closer we get, the harder will the forces of evil work to try and thwart our progress.[45] Please pardon my repeating: the idea is for us to *be with God*, and temptation is the opposing force aimed at interdicting our efforts in that regard. We need daily prayers for the wisdom to recognize temptation, to seek the grace to resist it, and to thank God for these necessary reinforcements!

We've already travelled no short distance together during our respective life-long earthbound relationships with our creator—while striving for an eternal reward the very pursuit of which can yield great joy. As we gravitate evermore closely to God, our enthusiasm should grow. Now is hardly a time for our daily thoughts of God to

---

45   "[W]hen I want to do what is good, evil lies close at hand" (Romans 7:19–25).

flag, or our love of God to fade. Take a deep cleansing breath, bear in mind that by going slow and steady you can win this race, and remember that heaven will wait!

Were I God,
my mind might immensely be muddled
by man(un)kind.

***Love** song, **love** story, **love** poem: the*
modifier; God's gift so badly misplaced,
losing its rightfully infinite space, along-
side grace.

Free will allows us our flirtations with fire,
drawn by warmth and dancing flames' pyre,
while love can be placid, even cool in desire.

*May I thrive for but **one second** on limitless,*
time-transcending, ever ascending heavenward
love.

Dealing with Doubt

Even the most faithful can sometimes harbor doubts. For any number of reasons—rational or otherwise—one's belief system can become shaken.

Have you lost a loved one, sustained some economic hardship, or fallen prey to illness . . . and asked why God allowed it to happen? Or, do wars and terrorist acts lead you to question God's very existence? Any experiences such as these can cause us to go through a weak patch in our faith journey. Whenever that happens, we are acutely at risk of drifting away from God. We have free will, which enables us to abandon God. So too do the war mongers, terrorists, and other evil-doers have free will. Bad things that happen are not God's fault. (Please re-read the last sentence . . . more than once, if necessary.) *How we react* to unfortunate occurrences *is our responsibility*.

What do you think it means when we ask God, in the Our Father (Lord's Prayer), to "lead us not into temptation"? Why would God ever "lead us into temptation"? Here's what those words are all about: God tests us, and in that quoted passage we're seeking relief from such trials, lest we fail to meet their challenge.[46] This is an opportunity to prove our love for God, as well as our trust in God. Don't turn away! It's all too common for those of us who teach upper-level courses to be asked by students whether certain material will be on the final exam, but when it comes to how we deal with misfortune, that actually *is* the exam!

✦

Maintaining a prayerful life isn't always easy. Self-awareness is especially important: Do you continue to believe in God, or have you given up on that idea altogether? Are you willing to examine your conscience in an effort to face up to what you've done—or failed to do—since your last confession? If so, go to confession and receive forgiveness; you'll be glad you did! Can you bring yourself to attend Mass? If so, arrive early rather than late. Receive Communion if you're free from mortal sin (don't count your current doubts as disqualifying), and seek God's grace for renewed faith.

---

46   *See* Peter Kreeft, *Fundamentals of the Faith: Essays in Christian Apologetics* (Ignatius Press, 1988), Pt. II ("Fundamentals of Christian Spirituality"), essay 36, 231–232.

The process is akin to bucking a strong headwind: you bend into it and plow ahead slowly in order to realize progress.

✦

My own drifting away wasn't caused by any personal doubts about God's existence. And yet, gradually God became ever less a part of my life as worldly pursuits and pleasures crowded God out. It seemed innocuous enough as my daily consciousness of God diminished. The distractions weren't necessarily sinful, either, although certainly some portion of them was, and that part perforce increased as time went by. Ultimately I stopped going to Mass. At that point, my regular awareness of and relationship with God were gone.

When we forget that there's more to this life than *just this life*, we miss out on the very best parts!

So, how was life for Bill during this protracted period of departure? Okay, I guess. Better than now? No, not even close! In a manner of speaking, I'd become fixated on an ever-changing array of shiny objects and flashy people. To be sure, illusions can at times seem magical; but they're not real. I hadn't gotten in too deep; rather, my life had become all too shallow. When we either forget or lose sight of the fact that there's so much more to this life than *just this life*, we miss out on the very best parts!

✦

Several years ago, when we were building a house in the woods of Westmoreland County, I was by myself there in the late afternoon of a comfortably warm day. Scrunched crosswise in the log cabin's back door jamb as the minor aches, pains, and fatigue from physical labor slowly subsided, I gazed into the woodland for nearly an hour. Just a few feet away, some months earlier, while I was fussing in the dirt with something or other, a strong force rushed past so near as to shake the ground about me. I looked up, and there stood the deer that must have missed me by inches, staring back. This afternoon, though, the same area of woods was completely clear of animate life—just towering trees with fluttering leaves and late-day sunrays filtering through. Those sublimely peaceful circumstances, free from harsh noise or other distraction, were conducive to my entering a semi-meditative state: the pure clarity of thought was inspirationally uplifting. Ultimately, I left for Pittsburgh convinced that no one with doubts could help but come to believe in God again, after sitting for a time where I had been. A nice thought—optimistic and possibly even wrong—yet it may be worth seeking out such peaceful circumstances, conducive to serene contemplation in times of doubt, for getting back in touch with God.

Looking across those very same woods now, on a cold and rainy mid-January day, is less inspiring. The trees and most vegetation are dormant, but they actually appear dead. Meager traces of greenery (pieris japonica, pachysandra, moss, a few stray evergreen saplings) faintly dot the predominantly gray-brown landscape. The overall message conveyed by this scene is more convincingly *mordant* than dormant; it's coldly colorless; only the *odor* of death is missing. I realize the big trees *are* still alive, despite their seeming not to be. Our soul may be likened to those trees' roots, always needing to be nourished and nurtured. Otherwise, we risk losing our life—the one that really counts: eternal life. Like tree roots, a good faith can become moribund without prayer.

In spring, those towering oak, maple, and hickory trees will leaf out. Above their topmost limbs majestic hawks will ride thermals while scanning the underbrush some hundred yards below in search of tasty tidbits. Then . . . then I will believe; it will be easier for me . . . then. There's only one question I must ask myself: Why not *now*?

For those of us fortunate enough to dwell where significant seasonal changes take place, a resurrection of sorts occurs each spring: what appeared outwardly to be dead during winter comes back to life in all fullness and glory. It's probably easier for most folks to feel that they're in the presence of God when spring bursts forth. First come the galanthus ("snow drops"), then crocus, followed by arrays of daffodils—all from the frost-gone ground. Some smaller understory trees start promising to break bud. These goings-on can (and should!) tend to dispel slight doubts as they convey a "God is with us" message. When we enthusiastically embrace the phenomena of nature,

their influence upon our belief system naturally increases. As stated in my Introduction, the idea is for us to *be with God*, which serves to *crowd out doubt*.

✦

During her entire adult life, Mother Theresa worried about whether God loved
her. The Holy Spirit continued to inspire her perseverance and maintain her hope
over the years. As we see from her saintly time on earth, doubt can prove to be an em-
powering force that draws us ever closer to God. So, if you ever find yourself doubt-
ing, take heart: one would be hard-pressed to follow in better footsteps than hers!

Distinctions

Navigating a course toward God should not prove particularly challenging on a day-to-day basis. It's not all that complicated! In the Beatitudes,[47] Christ provided us with a lifetime supply of behavior patterns for our personal improvement. The merciful, the peacemakers, the pure of heart, those who hunger and thirst for justice, and many others who—generally speaking—strive to improve the human condition, all stand to reap heavenly rewards. Moreover, Christ encourages us to embrace certain virtuous behaviors in respect of our fellow man: feed the hungry, clothe the naked, visit the sick, bury the dead, and in general love our neighbors as much as we love ourselves. The next few pages attempt to illuminate how those patterns can serve as pathways to God by briefly exploring a short list of fairly common conditions most of us are likely to encounter. We'll ease into this by first considering *subtleties*, before moving into *contrasts*.

Subtleties

As we strive to meet Christ's suggested markers along our way, slight shadings—nuances—can develop in our predominantly good behavior that could either beneficially augment or unfortunately compromise them to some extent.

<u>Compassion and Charity</u>

Compassion can result from becoming fully familiar with the plight of others and understanding the difficulties they face. Such awareness will tend to foster feelings of *empathy*, whereupon you're on the path toward becoming compassionate. The kind of understanding that involves knowing the heart of another—empathy—can be linked to acting ethically and morally. "We are more likely to treat other people

---

47   Matthew 5:1–12. *Cf.* Luke 6:20–26, where Beatitudes introduced with "Blessed are . . ." become coupled with a quartet introduced by "Woe to" (to wit, the "rich," those "filled now" who will be hungry, those laughing now who will "grieve and weep," and those of whom all "speak well . . . for their ancestors treated the false prophets that way"). Rather than pitting rich against poor, etc., as sometimes thought, those "woe to" are singled out for harboring an "eat, drink, and be merry" mindset that focuses on *this temporal life* without regard for acting selflessly.

well if we can find ways to empathize with them."[48] Unfortunately, as Pope Francis points out, ". . . a globalization of indifference has developed. Almost without being aware of it, we end up being incapable of feeling compassion at the outcry of the poor, weeping for other people's pain, and feeling a need to help them, as though all this were someone else's responsibility and not our own."[49]

Without a doubt, it can be easier to look away; discomfort is felt from another's pain and suffering. We need to resist this temptation to disregard, and instead try to walk a mile in the shoes of those less fortunate than ourselves. In theory, at least, compassion should inspire actions calculated to reduce or remove the adverse circumstances faced by others. Our goal, both individually and societally, ought be to restore and maintain the human dignity of anyone and everyone who's less fortunate. Otherwise, we are heartless.[50]

We all want to maintain (or, if need be, regain) our human dignity. Some individuals, although working for a living, cannot make ends meet. They face difficult compromises that can dilute their dignity. It's callous to think that such folks are themselves responsible for their unfortunate circumstances. Pope Francis is wont to ask, when observing the plight of the unfortunate, "Why them and not me?" As he has said, "I could have very well ended up among today's 'discarded people.'" Quite obviously, any of us could have been among the "discarded." To suggest that the impoverished take on a second or third job is both unrealistic and insensitive. We must not lose sight of the severe economic pressures faced by those in dire financial straits due to their being unemployed, underemployed, or underpaid. To maintain empathy, observe their plight in a clear-eyed manner with a realization that "there, but for the grace of God, go I."

Consider how Christ surrendered his dignity in order to restore ours. On the evening before Christ's crucifixion, he washed his apostles' feet. His passion and death

48   P. Salovey (President, Yale University), The Baccalaureate Address, May 20 and 21, 2017. See *Yale Alumni Magazine* (July/August 2017): 46.

49   Pope Francis, *Evangelii Gaudium*, Chapter 2, paragraph #54. © Libreria Editrice Vaticana, 2016.

50   See George Yancy, "Is Your God Dead?" Opinion, *The New York Times*, June 19, 2017, https://www.nytimes.com/2017/6/19/opinion/is-your-god-dead.html?emc=edit_th_20170619&nl=todaysheadlines&n-lid=50434725.

on the cross were the ultimate sacrifice. How dare we overlook those gifts he gave us so unselfishly, by either disregarding or disrespecting the dignity of our fellow man?

A vital aspect of "loving your neighbor as yourself" involves maintaining a compassionate attitude toward everyone else . . . in the world. The United States has long been considered the richest country in terms of wealth, but our place in history will be measured by whether or not we prove to be a compassionate nation.

When I was growing up, life on earth was frequently referred to in church circles as a "veil of tears." It's an expression less commonly heard these days. Make no mistake, for much of mankind that veil, and the tears, continue. Be compassionate; act compassionately. Of course, being compassionate typically entails blending in *charity*.[51]

> *Lord, teach me to be generous. Teach me to serve You as You deserve; to give and not to count the cost; to fight and not to heed the wounds; to toil and not to seek for rest; to labor and not to ask for reward, save that of knowing that I am doing Your will.*
>
> ~*Prayer of Generosity, St. Ignatius of Loyola*[52]

Forgiveness and Mercy

Forgiveness is necessary. There will always be conflicts, not all of which will be susceptible to ready compromise. Each party is likely then to think of the other as being at fault. At that juncture, they must both forgive and forget the conflict. Otherwise, it will fester, most likely grow, and yield no progress.

Be wary of a latent dark side to forgiveness. In the course of forgiving, one can inadvertently assert superiority. Figuratively speaking, forgiveness may manifest itself as all too akin to a pat on the head. Whereas "to forgive is divine" may well be true, the forgiveness must be free from any semblance of condescension.

---

51   During 2015, according to Giving USA, we donated $373.25 billion to charitable causes. Of that munificent sum, 80 percent was contributed by individual donors (versus foundations and corporations), which is most impressive. Even so, our problems of child poverty (20 percent of our children) and homelessness (half a million individuals) persist: "Still the children wander homeless,/ Still the hungry cry for bread." "Lord, Whose Love in Humble Service," by Albert F. Bayly (1901–1984), verse 2 (Oxford University Press, 1988). There are some "2.8 billion people in the world who subsist on less than $2 a day, and 1.2 billion of them on less than $1 a day," according to Myers and Kent, *The New Consumers* (Washington, DC: Island Press, 2013), 3.

52   Smith and Merz, *op. cit. supra*, n. 26, 57.

Another piece of baggage that can sometimes come with forgiveness involves an implicit assumption of being "in the right." Most times, when feeling offended by someone, we consider them to be "in the wrong." They may well be, but think about how rare are absolutes in our lives. Absolutely right and absolutely wrong answers seldom appeared on the many exams I've graded. The same is apt to be true whenever we take offense from another's words, deeds, or acts of omission. Is it so clear that they were completely and absolutely "in the wrong"? Isn't it more likely that extenuating circumstances imparted some ambiguity, or shading, to the situation?

When we forgive, it ought be with an appreciation that the one we forgive was not (or at least may not have been) completely and absolutely wrong. In other words, include some compassionate understanding with your forgiveness. Heed the prayerful words Christ provided to us when we ask God to "forgive us our trespasses [or debts] as we forgive those who trespass against us [our debtors]." Without a doubt, we're all desirous of God's forgiveness, but note from those words in the Lord's Prayer, that the forgiveness we get from God will mirror the forgiveness we extend to our trespassers/debtors. Every time we pray the Our Father (Lord's Prayer), we're actually asking God for that which we give to others in forgiveness, no more and no less . . . so it's obviously advantageous for us to be more forgiving!

Repeatedly in Catholic liturgy God is referred to as being "all merciful," and repeatedly do we beseech God to "have mercy on us." Our prayers for God's mercy will often go hand-in-hand with our begging for forgiveness. While it may be that forgiveness can harbor a dark side (as we have seen), it remains possible for us to diminish or possibly even banish that risk by blending *mercy* with our forgiveness.

✦

Contrasts

We're all familiar with "either/or" propositions; they crop up frequently. The following distinctions aren't necessarily of that ilk, however. Take, for example, the first pair, "loving and fearing," both of which can coexist in our emotions respecting God. Because *fright* tends to trigger a *flight* response—we run away—while love draws us near, my instinct is to love rather than fear God. That said, a *just* God—who will mete out justice to the defiant—deserves to be accorded our full respect, which includes a modicum of fear. Consider the ensuing collection of contrasted pairings from the perspective of how compatible the two are with each other. It varies.

Loving versus Fearing

It is said that we cannot love someone whom we fear, and in a similar vein, we must trust someone in order to love them. With respect to God, the trust part should come easy,[53] but what about fear of the Almighty?

The Act of Contrition recites our "dread," which is to say *fear*, of losing heaven and suffering the pains of hell. Given such fears, can we still love God? Absolutely! Loving God should banish all fear of death and judgment—but *should* doesn't always come true.

We cannot hide from God, after all; God knows as well as we do how we comport ourselves during this life. (Because we're often prone to making excuses or giving alibis, God actually knows how we've behaved better than we ourselves do!) Any fear of God we feel ought be taken as a signal that we need to develop greater love for God by more rigorously obeying the Commandments, more lovingly embracing the Beatitudes, and, in general, living life more religiously. Let your growing love of God gradually eclipse those fears, and you'll lead a better, happier life on earth while heaven awaits.

Self-Sufficiency versus Dependence

For many of us, I think it's fair to say, there are three periods in our lives when we strive mightily to gain or maintain self-sufficiency: early youth, young adulthood, and older age. When our firstborn child Will was very young, he would evidence this desire for independence by claiming, "I am big to do that job." Now in his late twenties, like so many of his young-adult peers (including his younger brother Brendan),

---

53   Some individuals who suffer grave loss or are exposed to catastrophe or betrayed by someone close to them may blame God for not intervening to prevent their hardship and suffering. It will be necessary for them to move beyond the resulting feelings of devastation before becoming able to trust in God again. In his book, *Finding God in All Things* (Ave Maria, 1991), William A. Barry, SJ devotes an entire chapter to such efforts: "Can I Trust God: Healing Life's Hurts," 21–32. I beg those who reacted with even the slightest hesitation to my assertion that trust in God "should come easy" to carefully, closely peruse those pages.

Will wants to be out on his own, no longer under his parents' wings. And finally—the voice of my experience here—as we advance in years, we struggle against becoming dependent upon others for help.

I was in my late thirties, living comfortably with a secure teaching job, when my mother died in December of 1977. The mad scramble of handing her funeral in Pittsburgh and burial arrangements on Staten Island, New York, rapidly threw me into a newfound state of necessary self-sufficiency. Without doubt, my mother was the strongest religious influence in my life—even more so than twenty years of Catholic schooling. She led me toward God, teaching me by example. After her death, I was depressed, naturally. But more than that (and unknowingly) I suffered from spiritual desolation. At some point, not very long after she died, my drift away from God and church began. I maintained *self-sufficiency*—was not at all dependent—just when I should have been leaning on God for help. From a religious standpoint I became *complacent*, and therein lies the problem!

Recognize that self-sufficiency emphasizes *self*. In contrast, Christ led a selfless life on earth, just as our own prayerful moments are necessarily selfless. No matter how self-sufficient we may desire to be, it's critically important never to lose sight of our dependency upon God. I remained a "fallen-away Catholic" for many years following my mother's death, extending through my courtship of, engagement to, and marriage with Eliza (a faithful Presbyterian), the births of our three children, and even their early upbringing. Once on the "self" track, it's not easy to get off. There were times of selflessness, of course, as would naturally be expected of any man with a sweet wife and good children, notwithstanding his predominantly selfish behavior. All told, there was no real dependency on my part toward anyone else. That was not good.

Dependency isn't so bad; it's clearly just pride that tends to make us loathe dependency. And that should tell you something: pride isn't especially good!

We remain dependent upon God *for our entire life*. Because of that (and for innumerable other reasons) we should love God always and in all ways. Beware of those instances in life when greater self-sufficiency is demanded of you by special circumstances. Rising to those occasions and braving through them may be admirable, but at the same time it's important to maintain a lifelong love of God in our hearts, a realization of our dependency upon God for grace to nourish our souls, and an ongoing awareness of our need to keep praying.

Solitude versus Loneliness

Being the more sociable member of our partnership, Eliza is energized by being with people, while at the same time I can be getting fatigued. In large groups I'll nearly always behave like a pilot fish swimming by her side. It's a good balance when we're together; I love being with her "apart from the maddening crowd." Just now, writing while Eliza's at work and Knox sleeps, might pass for "solitude"; it's certainly far from loneliness. Like some of the other distinctions being drawn here, solitude isn't so bad, whereas loneliness is undesirable. But the attractive aspect of this pairing is that *both* solitude and loneliness can afford us opportunities to grow closer to God!

The Beatles (no less) referred to "all the lonely people," and asked "where do they all come from?" Being unsure of how to answer that, allow me to suggest where so many lonely people *go*, or end up: nursing homes, similar life-care facilities, and hospitals. Visiting restrictions are imposed by some of these institutions (especially hospitals), but most welcome friends to come in . . . and strangers, too, on occasion. For example, our daughter Regina played violin with a small orchestra while she was in grammar school, and the group would perform from time to time at care facilities in and about Pittsburgh.

One of the virtues depicted graphically on the stone floor of the main aisle in Sacred Heart Church (my parish in Pittsburgh) lauds visiting the sick. No doubt it's as virtuous to visit the lonely. Any time we can make a lonely person smile, we should; God will likely smile upon us for doing so!

This can sometimes be a tough gig: visiting my father was difficult due to his depressing surroundings while in a nursing home. Early in the afternoon of the day before Dad died, his body was riddled with bed sores (nickel-sized ovals of raw-looking flesh bereft of epidermal protection). I pleaded with the head nurse, Bonita, to help him. "There's nothing we can do," she said, and accurately predicted that my father's end was near. Years before, when Dad first became too much for my mother to handle solo, Bonita had helped take care of him at home. Back then, if he were left at home alone, it was solitude; in the nursing home, that had soured into loneliness. Circumstances, coupled with one's individual outlook, can slant a given situation toward either solitude or loneliness; it depends. Especially during his last summer, when my mother was hospitalized due to a nearly fatal heart attack (something Dad could never fathom), he was lost in loneliness without her.

Nursing homes tend to be brighter nowadays. Visits to Eliza's parents, at least while they continued living together in a latter-day care facility, could be uplifting. It helped a great deal that Liza and her brother had cleverly furnished their parents' nursing home rooms with furniture and furnishings selected from the parents' former home of fifty years. This minimized the adjustment involved in their moving.

✦

For many of us, solitude has become a rare commodity in today's workaday world. We need to make an effort to set aside some time to contemplate, without distraction. A good beginning is to think about God's gifts to us . . . good graces we've received most recently as well as back in time. These thoughts will foster feelings of personal happiness, contentment, and gratitude to God. Then, ask what it is that God most wants of you; seek God's guidance for finding your personal path to goodness. Does it feel like you're praying? Well, you are!

Doing Good versus Doing Well

Last night, my first-born son was feeling discouraged.

Will's efforts to sell break-through technology to homeowners (who would realize savings on their electric utility bills) weren't panning out. Other sales people, who had backgrounds in selling cable television and internet access services, were out-performing him. There were techniques they used, with evident success, that made Will uncomfortable . . . so he refused to incorporate them into his sales pitch. In consequence, he was not doing so *well* as he wished. At the same time, he made me glow with pride by choosing to be *good*. He decided, as a matter of conscience, to be an altogether forthright salesman by emphasizing honesty and making ethical judgments. It is not easy to do *good* when that can only be achieved at the cost of not doing so *well* financially. God bless you, Will, for choosing the better path.

Fights versus Arguments

My pastor, Father Robert Grecco, related to me this difference between arguing and fighting:

Fights produce a victor, or winner, as well as a loser. In interpersonal relationships, however, neither person who emerges from a fight is likely better off. In the interest of preserving domestic tranquility, whether within our families or among our friends, fights are to be avoided like the plague.

Arguments aren't so bad. Not that it's likely anyone would relish a steady diet of argumentation, but at least these natural confrontations are not generally calculated to produce a winner and a loser. It's possible to *settle* an argument, whereas the only comparable end to a fight may well involve someone having to throw in the towel.

The distinction being drawn here is not merely a semantic one. The winner/loser aftermath from a fight leaves both combatants wounded. Worse, little if any progress will have been made toward their reaching an accord. Arguments, on the other hand, are far less about beating someone down.

When properly conducted and concluded, an argument can even strengthen the relationship between the parties. For an argument to be productive in this way, though, extraneous clutter must be kept off the table. There's a need to stay focused on the point in contention. Avoid muddying the waters with matters not integral to that point.

Look forward to a handshake, a hug, or perhaps—if need be—an agreement not to agree!

Most if not all of us have encountered an "irreconcilable conflict" in the course of our lives. An approach for addressing such situations appears in the Gospel of Matthew (18:15-17), where Jesus is reported to have said to his disciples: "If your brother sins against you, go and tell him his fault between you and him alone. If he listens to you, you have won over your brother. If he does not listen, take one or two others along with you, so that every fact may be established on the testimony of two or three witnesses. If he refuses to listen to them, tell the Church. If he refuses to listen even to the Church, then treat him as you would a Gentile or a tax collector." I long misunderstood those final words to mean that, if all efforts fail to bring someone around, treat them with disdain. Fortunately, this morning's homily by Father Thomas Gramc at St. Paul Cathedral set me straight: To Jesus, the Gentiles and tax collectors were candidates for conversion (rather than derision)! It's worth noting that this Gospel is written by Matthew, who himself was once a tax collector—before becoming a convert to Christ!

Be thankful for the uncomfortable, unpleasant,
and ever-undesired, as from them do we become
Able to see God — the light, truth, and way —
when reaching out,

for . . .

Unless we have
pain in our lives,
How hard it will be
to feel others' agony.

About Praying

Imagine that you had to deliver an important message to someone. A message so important that you first prepared the precise language to say, and then memorized those words. Now comes the critical moment when you actually deliver your well-chosen words. It will undercut your message significantly if you merely *recite* what you have memorized. In that case, you will be talking *at* the listener. This can happen when praying, regardless of whether you pray aloud or to yourself, and whether you're asking for assistance or giving thanks.

When we say prayers such as the Hail Mary, Our Father (Lord's Prayer), or even an Act of Contrition, the words are usually coming from deep in our memory. This actually poses something of a challenge. Rather than a recitation, our prayers should be conversational. A modicum of care must therefore be taken, in order to speak *with* God when saying prayers that we know by heart.

Our world is often so cluttered—whether by noise, events happening around us, or other distractions—that it can sometimes be difficult to maintain focus throughout a prayer. Thoughts about extraneous matters may cross our mind ("remember to . . ."), interrupting the prayer we're trying to say. I think it's generally preferable to start over when that happens. The more often you do so, the greater may become your resistance to having subsequent prayers interrupted by distractions. Always be fully engaged during your prayerful moments, as a matter of basic respect, and don't monopolize the conversation—listen to/for God!

About your prayerful moments: It's a worthy objective to expand the circumstances under which you pray. Morning and evening prayers, grace before and after meals, are all fine and good—but there's so much more. For example, if you have a snack between meals, consider saying a shorthand "thank you, God" as grace. Suppose your night's sleep is interrupted for some reason; why not consider repeating your evening prayers when returning to bed? Since prayer is simply a matter of turning your mind and heart to God, there's no need for a preplanned script or lengthy oration here. Just say, or contemplate, whatever words come naturally to you. *Improvise!* When walking the dog . . . pray. Commuting to work . . . pray. Make the occasional mindless intervals in your day a time for prayer. ***Be opportunistic!***

It's a worthy objective to expand the circumstances under which you pray.

Many of us may think "prayer" involves, for the most part, reciting familiar scripts long held deep in memory. While this view of prayer is hardly incorrect, we can benefit from broadening the *scope* of our praying. A beautiful conceptualization was articulated by the "Little Flower" (St. Thérèse of Lisieux—youngest doctor of the church): "prayer is a surge of the heart; it is a simple look turned toward heaven; it is a cry of recognition and of love, embracing both trial and joy." Just think how much more of each and every day could incorporate prayer, by our simply embracing this view!

Every now and then I'll think of an old friend, someone gone or nearly forgotten. And because they've crossed my mind, I may feel inclined to say a prayer for them right then. Wherever they are, on earth or afar, perhaps they'll return the favor just when I'm in need of it most. Never can tell. . . .

Several days ago a local supermarket was promoting licorice sales by positioning bags full of those thin, black licorice tubes right next to the check-out counter. Because my mother loved licorice, she came to mind, so I said a Hail Mary for my mother. Moments later, when leaving the store, I crossed paths with a young man whose black tee-shirt bore the words "daily bread." Time for an Our Father! You get the idea. . . .

Finally, if your place of worship provides them, read the lyrics to hymns from the hymnal. (It's even better if you can read music!). You will quickly recognize that hymns are lyrical prayers to be embraced with pleasure. In a similar vein have I found inspiration by reading *Love Poems from God*.[54] Hymns and religious poems alike can add a new dimension to your praying.

✦

---

54   *Love Poems from God: Twelve Sacred Voices from the East and West*, trans. Daniel Ladinsky (New York: Penguin, 2002).

Isn't it likely that the greatest beauty we behold in this world—whether the fall colors of deciduous trees, a spectacular sunset, or rainbows—will be far exceeded in the next life?

Over the past few years, I participated in a couple of art workshops—one for oil painting, the other, pastels—and while my own work may not have improved so much, the way I *see* things has; the breathtaking beauty of God's creativity often escaped my purview previously, but far less so now. An even greater quantum leap is likely to be in store during our transition from this to the next life.

If you've never thought of yourself as dancing with God, singing a duet with God, or even enjoying a joke with God, loosen up! I'm not being disrespectful here; our appreciation of music and humor must surely come from God. It underestimates and probably even insults our creator to think of God as "stodgy." In the same vein, regarding prayer, don't wait: speak with God more openly, more excitedly, without inhibitions. ***Start Today!***

I think you'll find it pleasantly surprising how much these various practices can *elevate your spirits*. Realizing this goal requires only that you introduce prayer into your day-to-day being. Try it for a while; you'll probably come to agree.

✦

Two approaches to prayer were unfamiliar to me before beginning to write this book:

In Benedictine monasteries, a practice known as the Divine Office is observed (similar to the Office prayed daily by priests, nuns, and others in religious life). Macrina Wiederkehr offers us a layman's version of such practices in her book, *Seven Sacred Pauses: Living Mindfully Through the Hours of the Day*,[55] a beautiful blend of accessible spiritual writings, including scripture and poetry.

The heritage of Saint Ignatius of Loyola, founder of the Jesuit order, includes a sixteenth-century work known as *The Spiritual Exercises*. I benefit from being guided through the *Exercises* by regular meetings with Sister Carole Riley, PhD, Executive Director of the West Virginia Institute for Spirituality. She supervises my contempla-

---

55   Macrina Wiederkehr, *Seven Sacred Pauses: Living Mindfully Through the Hours of the Day* (Notre Dame, IN: Sorin, 2008).

tion of one "Moment" each week, from the book *Moment by Moment: A Retreat in Everyday Life*, by Carol Ann Smith and Eugene F. Merz.[56]

✦

The most intense prayer context may well be that presented by a retreat. Typically, retreats involve a group (sometimes referred to as "retreatants"), before whom one or more speakers will address the particular subject of that retreat. A retreat can also be self-conducted, however, which would usually entail following a format written by someone experienced in presenting retreats to groups (for example, Macrina Wiederkehr's "Behold Your Life," published by Ave Maria Press). My high school, Augustinian Academy on Staten Island, New York, produced a one-day "silent" retreat (students were expected to maintain silence during the retreat) annually for all students. I can still recall a story told by one of those speakers—more than sixty years ago! Retreats can be memorable, moving experiences, and they're currently enjoying a resurgence in popularity.

✦

We've progressed, in the course of this little book, from a "learn from my mistakes" approach to your gradually fostering a fortress of faith through prayer. What lies in store from your continuing to draw ever more close to God is *the most intense joy you can possibly experience during this life.* You just have to supply the means, respect the process, and give it time.

---

56   Ibid.

Mary

Apart from the "Hail Mary pass" that crops up mostly in reference to football, the Mother of God receives little attention outside Catholicism. Regardless of how, or even whether, you may think of the Blessed Mother, please take a couple of minutes to learn a little bit about the prayer most often said to her. Its name is derived from the opening salutation, "Hail, Mary . . . full of grace."

This short and simple prayer to Mary contains just three parts: first is the Angel Gabriel's annunciation to Mary that "the Lord is with Thee" (meaning that she is pregnant, carrying the Son of God); next are the complimentary greetings from her cousin Elizabeth, "Blessed art thou among women, and blessed is the fruit of thy womb, Jesus"; and the final eighteen words, standing alone, are themselves a beautiful little prayer: "Holy Mary, mother of God, pray for us sinners now and at the hour of our death, Amen." (For better or worse, I sometimes envision Michelangelo's "Pieta" sculpture during that last phrase.)

Before considering several other prominent prayers to Mary, it may be worthwhile for us to fill in some background to the Hail Mary. When the "Annunciation" occurred, Mary was quite young, without carnal knowledge of any man: a virgin. Thus the role into which Mary was being cast seemed to her impossible to fill, and she said as much to the Angel Gabriel. Since she was being conceived of the Holy Spirit, according to God's will, however, Mary accepted with characteristic grace: "Be it done unto me according to Thy word." Soon thereafter, eager to share this miraculous event with her elder cousin Elizabeth (who, the Angel Gabriel had informed Mary, was also pregnant), Mary set out from Nazareth to visit her. Elizabeth and her husband, Zachary, lived in a small town, Ain Karim, in the hill country of Judah, nearly 100 miles away (Luke 1:39). By grace of God, coupled with the determination of her own will, Mary reached her cousin. Although previously thought "barren"(incapable of child bearing), Elizabeth was already in her sixth month when Mary arrived. The embryonic boy then developing in Elizabeth's womb reacted to Mary's presence (Luke 1:41 and 44-45), presaging the historically significant relationship that lay in store between him—John the Baptist, *en ventre sa mere*—and Jesus. Mary stayed with Elizabeth for some time before returning home. Meanwhile, Joseph, to whom Mary was betrothed, received angelic counsel against rejecting Mary because of her pregnancy. Recalling these origins of the Hail Mary prayer should make it considerably easier for you to avoid lapsing into rote recitations. We need to strive for prayerful conversations, rather than just reciting memorized words, in order for us to draw closer to God.

All told, from when Mary was called upon to carry the Christ child in her womb, to when she cradled her son after he had died on a Calvary cross, Mary must have experienced a greater range of emotions than any other human being ever. If you feel intensely close to God (as I do) when receiving the Holy Eucharist, consider Mary: our intimacy with Jesus, while the host is in our mouth and body, lasts for only a relatively brief time; Mary carried Christ in her body for nine months! Because she was human, I find Mary readily approachable, and I pray the Hail Mary with some regularity.

Another prayer to Mary—customarily said at noontime (also at 6:00 p.m.)—is the beautiful Angelus. The first two lines of that prayer are: "The Angel of the Lord declared unto Mary / and she was conceived of the Holy Ghost." These words are followed by a Hail Mary, and then two more pairs of lines with Hail Mary after, plus a brief closing prayer. My college had an enormous old pedestal-mounted bell in the center of campus that was rung every day at noon for the Angelus: *Suenen Campanos!*[57] Everyone stopped and said the prayer to themselves before returning to pedestrian matters. It was a nice tradition, and pretty stirring.

Any parent or teacher desirous of introducing a young child to prayer could do well to consider a poem my own mother spoke to me: "Lovely Lady Dressed in Blue," by Mary Dixon Thayer.[58] As its first line continues, "teach me how to pray. God was just your little boy, so you know the way." Of course, this beautiful poem is itself a prayer! With all due respect to George Gershwin's magnificent musical composition, penned in 1924, I cannot help but think of the Blessed Mother, Virgin Mary, as the *original* "Rhapsody in Blue."

---

57   Hymn, "Joyous Bells," in *Worship*, #518.
58   www.catholictradition.org/Mary/lady.htm.

When you're ready for greater devotion to Mary, consider praying the Rosary. (Just be sure that you continue paying attention to the history and meaning of words in the Hail Mary, without allowing yourself to lapse into rote recitals. Each and every time you say/pray a Hail Mary, be consciously aware of its three parts: Gabriel's greeting/announcement, Elizabeth's praises, and your own petition.) A most helpful booklet is "How to Pray the Holy Rosary," published by Lighthouse Catholic Media.[59] As you probably know, rosary beads are strung in sets of ten (a "decade"), with a distinguishable (either larger, or differently colored) bead spaced between each decade for praying an Our Father. A complete rosary, comprising five decades, is recited to commemorate one out of the four categories of mysteries—joyful, luminous, sorrowful, and glorious—which are designated for different days of the week (sometimes called a "scriptural rosary").

I may be accused of having saved the best for last: the Canticle of Mary, thought to be the most ancient hymn to Mary, is also known as the Song to Mary, or Magnificat. Its words are from Mary's response to her cousin Elizabeth, whose praises of Mary are included in the Hail Mary. Basically, Mary responds, "my soul magnifies the Lord." This hymn is either sung or recited, typically as part of the evening prayer service known as Vespers or Evensong. It's lovely.

✦

Inasmuch as most Catholics tend to say (or recite) three prayers more than all others—the Hail Mary, Our Father, and Glory Be (prayer to the Holy Trinity)—let's conclude by focusing briefly on those two prayers often paired with the Hail Mary.

The Our Father enjoys universal popularity as a prayer among all Christians, which is only fitting inasmuch as the words came to us from Christ.[60] (There's good reason why it's known as the Lord's Prayer!) In a brief homily during morning Mass at Sacred Heart Church on the first Tuesday in Lent (2017), Father Robert Grecco made a great suggestion: that we contemplate one line or phrase from the Our Father each day as a Lenten devotion.

---

59   www.LighthouseCatholicMedia.org.
60   Matthew 6:7–13.

Earlier this week (on September 26, 2017) during our 8:30 Mass, Father Grecco preached to several of the earlier classes of young students from Sacred Heart Elementary School. The Gospel (Matthew 6:7–13) was in the form presented by the Contemporary English Version of the American Bible Society's missal, written for fourth graders. (Father Grecco told me afterward that Sacred Heart school children attending that Mass were more advanced, already knowing the words to the Our Father by heart—and thus tended to get confused by this missal's considerably simplified language.) In that Gospel passage, Matthew recounts when Christ gave us the Lord's Prayer, or Our Father. (Back when the use of Latin was considerably more prevalent in Catholic worship, it was also known as the *Pater Noster*.) As our pastor pointed out to the children, it is significant that Christ's words characterize God the Father as *our* father. By becoming man, Christ eradicated the sins of our earliest parents on earth; his death and resurrection gave us new life; and as the prayer he gave us discloses, his father is likewise *our* father.

During childhood, most of us disobeyed our parents on occasion (if not more regularly). After a beloved, previously disrespected parent dies, it is painful for us to recall instances when we wronged them. Our regrets may well be coupled with a wish that we could return to the time when our parents were still living, so we could demonstrate love for them through unfailing obedience. Although we don't get to relive those times past, God is *our father* now and forever. An opportunity still exists to show our love by living the rest of our days as he wishes. Appreciate each and every word of this prayer, including the first two—Our Father—and let the fullness of their meaning sink in.

Rather than attempting to explain this prayer's elements, I'll defer to Boston College Professor Peter Kreeft, who has already done so far better than I ever could.[61] I dare say, you'll never say/pray an Our Father the same again, after reading Professor Kreeft's analysis of this prayer Christ gave us.

✦

---

61   See *Fundamentals of the Faith: Essays in Christian Apologetics* (Ignatius, 1988), Pt. II ("Fundamentals of Christian Spirituality"), essays 31–36, 189–239.

Several months ago, while Eliza and I were walking with our long-time friend Carl Katz (who admits to being more spiritual than religious), he incidentally asked why a "Holy Ghost" was included in most Christian denominations. (The exception is Unitarians, whose tenets do not include the Holy Trinity.) The best theory I've heard to explain *existence* of the Holy Ghost is that God loves himself, thereby causing the Son to exist, and in turn the Spirit (or Holy Ghost) constitutes the love between them. As for the *role* of the Holy Ghost, we need only reference scripture; the Spirit is alluded to with some frequency as the source of man's enlightenment about God, religion, and what God wants of us. (In all candor, I couldn't compose these writings without substantial spiritual help. Should you come upon good messages herein, know that I had a ghostwriter and credit the Spirit.)

I accept as a matter of faith that the Father, the Son, and the Holy Spirit exist as one God in three divine "persons." This is the *triune* in which Catholics believe.[62] Nature affords us a useful Holy Trinity analogy: the *trifolium*, or three-leafed clover (after which we named our woodland retreat, *Trifol*). A common prayer to the Holy Trinity is: "Glory be to the Father, and to the Son, and to the Holy Spirit, as it was in the beginning, is now, and ever shall be, world without end, Amen."[63] Yet more basic is the Sign of the Cross, which is often accompanied by holy water (where available) as a form of renewing our baptism.

While walking back to my car after this morning's 8:30 Mass at Sacred Heart, I saw two young men riding their bikes down Emerson Street, across Walnut. On the northeast corner of that intersection lies Sacred Heart Church and Elementary School. Without slowing his pace, the lead biker made the Sign of the Cross. God bless him!

---

62   For more about the Trinity—to which early Christians applied the Greek word *perichoresis* (meaning, in essence, *dancing*)—consider Fr. Richard Rohr (with Mike Morrell), *The Divine Dance, The Trinity and Your Transformation* (New Kensington, PA: Whitaker House, 2016).

63   By my linguistically referencing "persons" and this prayer's reference to "beginning," we yet again confirm the limitations of our perceptions as finite, physical creatures.

The End

Death, thou wast once an uncouth, hideous thing,
But since our Savior's death did put some blood into thy face;
Thou art grown fair and full of grace,
Much in request, much sought for as a good.

George Herbert[64]

Death marks the end of our life on earth, and this twenty-fifth essay constitutes the last in my *Canticle*, but there's so much left to say—thoughts that are anything but lineal—I beg your indulgence before we part.

Death is a reality far more certain and inevitable than taxes—despite that Benjamin Franklin tended to equate the two. Numerous alternatives to "death" and "dying" in our English language disclose a measure of uneasiness (or could it be preoccupation?) with this topic. Until now, I've made only vague references in this book to "when the music stops." Similarly, when teaching Federal Estate & Gift Taxation one semester, I employed other such euphemisms exclusively during the entire course: "kicked the bucket," "bought the farm," Citizen Kane's final "Rosebud" utterance, and many others. This became a source of humor as the course went along. But some individuals treat death so seriously that they refrain from writing a Last Will and Testament because it would necessitate facing the reality of their mortality. (I've suggested that any law student who encounters such a client should tell them, "If you're carrying an umbrella, it probably won't rain!")

Rather than being *fearful of death*, we ought to be *frightened of sin*. Once we appreciate that, the rest is obvious: we'll be prepared for death if we remain free from sin. If we can maintain a prayerful lifestyle without slips, trips, or errors . . . and whenever a stumble does occur, turn in haste to the Sacrament of Reconciliation . . . our fear of dying should be significantly diminished.

Panic set in as I checked each and every confessional at St. Paul Cathedral on that Holy Saturday when I resolved to return to God through the Sacrament of Reconciliation: "It's Saturday. This is when confessions are always heard. What's going on?

---

64   "Death," lines 1 and 13–16, from *The Temple, op. sit. supra*, n. 41.

Why is this place deserted?" Beyond feeling frustration, I was fearful. When it comes to saving your soul, fear can sometimes serve as a motivating influence. I wasn't really concerned about dying; it was unavailability of the Sacrament that worried me.

✦

There's an expression (probably dating back to World War I) to the effect that you'll never find an atheist in a foxhole. While never an atheist myself, the many fearful, death-defying moments in my life failed to turn me back toward God. Airborne in a rotary-engined Mazda Rx7; shearing the front end off a Raymond Lowey-designed Studebaker coupe (all the way back to the windshield); launched many yards by the car that struck as I began to cross a slushy street one mid-winter night in Poughkeepsie, New York; and (beyond battling two cancers and repeated blood clots) harboring a 99%-occluded coronary artery . . . none of them drew me back to God after I'd aimlessly drifted away. Rather, it was that then-nameless priest (Father Sodini) looking quizzically into my hospital room just before I underwent a scary, science-fiction sort of surgery: he did the trick! Why, I don't know, but that hardly matters. Once turned around, the dominating force in my life is a deep love of God.

God wants us to maintain ourselves in a state of grace—and loving God entails pleasing God by avoiding sin. Prayer is the best preventative measure against sinning. In my experience, the fear of death—even when felt while in dire danger—is ineffective (although plenty enervating!).

✦

Today is Good Friday (2017), and it's early spring in Rector, Pennsylvania, where *Trifol* (our woodland retreat house) is located. Countless daffodils are in bloom. Two redbuds that get good sun are as well. Small birds are merrily gamboling from the redbuds' branches to a nearby Cleveland Pear that's yet to flower, and a relatively tiny tree hydrangea (my one compromise with God's design) just starting to leaf. A white butterfly flutters by. Eliza sits next to me, working on a poem in honor of Dan Aleshire's retirement as long-term head of The Association of Theological Schools, and Knox is nearly asleep on the wicker chair next to her. I'm not thinking of dying, myself, but death is on my mind while writing . . . because this is the day when Christ died for us: "*Dies irae, dies illa / Solvet saeclum in favilla*" (Day of wrath and doom impending. heaven and earth in ashes ending).[65] As I dwell on Christ's death this most holy Friday, my mind is being riddled with thoughts of recent violence, devastation, and dying.

The United States dropped a 21,000-pound bomb yesterday, Holy Thursday (2017). It was the largest non-atomic explosive force in history. The target: an underground stronghold of ISIS terrorists near Kabul. The Middle East is littered with war zones, overrun with fleeing refugees. Some of these conflicts are considered *civil war*, others a form of *holy war*, both of which labels sound to me like oxymorons.

Christ did not die for this. He defeated death and soul-killing sin for us, but surely not for this.

✦

The ancient "eye for an eye" Code of Hammurabi apparently remains in play while Christ's counsel to "turn the other cheek" is relatively seldom being heard.[66] Christ opens his arms wide to welcome us, yet we fixate instead on arming for war (albeit called "defense spending"). Steadfastly claiming that "God is on our side," nations portray their arsenals of weapons as but deterrents against conflict. (It's a contention that smacks of familiar faulty logic: the more guns are owned by the public, the fewer shootings there'll be.) Far as I am from being an optimist, it may be the forthcoming resurrection of Christ that brings a certain hymn's lyrics to mind: "Could the world be about to turn?"[67] This train of thought continued over the weekend.

✦

The recessional hymn for Easter Sunday Mass at Sacred Heart Church was "Sing with All the Saints in Glory":

65 Dating back to about 1250 or earlier, this Latin funeral hymn now tends only to be heard on All Souls' Day (November 2nd). Negative spirituality from the Middle Ages, stressing despair and fear of Judgment Day, was generally discarded by the Second Vatican Council in favor of more positive messages emphasizing hope and the Resurrection of Christ. As I recall from singing in St. Peter's choir more than sixty-five years ago, however, it was the most dramatic piece of music on our Good Friday program.

66 Matthew 5: 38–40. *See also* 43–48, where Jesus said, "love your enemies and pray for those who persecute you, that you may be children of your heavenly Father, for he makes his sun rise on the bad and the good, and causes rain to fall on the just and the unjust."

67 Hymn "Canticle of the Turning," by Rory Cooney (b. 1952), to the traditional Irish folk tune, "Star of the County Down," in *Worship*, #624.

Death and sorrow, earth's dark story, / To the former days belong. /... In God's likeness, we awaken, / Knowing everlasting peace.[68]

Further to this, the stirring lyrics to Jean Sibelius' soaring *Finlandia* came to mind:

So hear my song, O God of all the nations, / A song of peace for their land and for mine.[69]

We need to live with *love*; we need to be at *peace*; *dona nobis pachem*.

Consider these lyrics from the hymn, "Prayer for Peace," based on a Navaho (Native American) tribal prayer:

Peace before us, peace behind us, peace under our feet. / Peace within us, peace over us, let all around us be peace.[70]

✦

Reality intrudes. Our nation's "defense" budget, nudging toward $600 billion annually, makes up approximately one-third of the total federal budget and more than half of federal discretionary spending (54 percent in 2015). It amounts to more than the next seven nations' defense budgets *combined*.

Christians, lay down your weapons of might;
Stock-piles but lead to terror and fright.[71]

Yet we hear (and some even cheer) Presidential promises of increased defense spending. Without in any way suggesting that the United States' already-weak wall between church and state be further compromised, I can't help wondering just how much we budget for *love of neighbor*.

✦

---

68   Hymn, text by William J. Irons (1812–1883), in *Worship #526*.

69   Hymn, "This is My Song," text by Lloyd Stone (1912–1993), verse 2, final bars, ©Lorenz Publishing Co., in *Worship*, #997. I recently came upon a wonderful hymn, also set to the score of Finlandia: "When Memory Fades," by Mary Louise Bringle (b.1953). The lyrics prayerfully address aging and its effects upon our physical condition, beginning with: "When mem'ry fades and recognition falters / When eyes we love grow dim, and minds, confused, / Speak to our souls of love that never alters; / Speak to our hearts by pain and fear abused," in *Worship*, #971.

70   Hymn, text by David Haas (b. 1957), © 1987, GIA Publications, Inc., in *Gather*, #305.

71   Hymn, "Jesus Still Lives," Suzanne Toolan, SM 1927, verse 2, ©1985 World Library Publications, Inc., in *Gather*, #302.

Meanwhile, our country's mounting gap between those in the most favorable financial circumstances and nearly everyone else (comprising the vast majority of our population) has drawn critical attention from Pope Francis. He properly regards "trickle down" economics as an approach that "has never been confirmed by the facts." Nonetheless, reductions in the extent of government-subsidized medical care for those who can least afford it, and tax cuts calculated to inure to those already rich, continue to be espoused and proposed with patently unrealistic increases in predicted revenue collections and economic growth being cited as justification. Do we not know any better, or do we just want to pretend not to know?

It's time to abandon these pernicious political policies in favor of profoundly prayerful practices. That should be the end . . . which is to say, our primary objective.

✦

Final thoughts: Imagine you were somehow made aware of when you would die and found out that your death was fairly imminent. Hard to imagine who would choose to sin under such circumstances, isn't it?!! Of course, this a far-fetched scenario for most of us (save for those *in extremis*), so let's return to normal. Though we know neither the day nor the hour of our death, I suspect that most of us realize (if only subconsciously) *there'll come a day* when we will indeed regret our sins.

It's always regrettable, whenever we fail,
to be as God's wish for our lives to avail.

Our feelings of regret may not set in, however, until much later on—long after we've strayed from God's wishes.

We then may regret or better yet repent,
such earlier hours . . . so badly mis-spent.

John Greenleaf Whittier, in "Maud Muller," poetically characterizes *worldly* regrets with these familiar lines:

For of all sad words of tongue or pen,
The saddest are these: "It might have been!"[72]

---

72   *Yale Book of American Verse* (1912), #76, verse 105.

Then W. H. Auden's poem, "The Cave of Making," considers how one might come to experience *spiritual* regrets:

God may reduce you
on Judgement Day
to tears of shame,
reciting by heart
the poems you would
have written, had
your life been good.[73]

We know that regrets will be in store
When the life we're living is no more . . .

And they will be, all, bitter pills to swallow,
Unless we, right now, reject a life so hollow:

Devote your life to God; pray Him to follow.

---

73   *About the House* (New York: Random House, 1965), from the "Thanksgiving for a Habitat" sequence of poems; in particular, "The Cave of Making" memorializes Louis MacNeice.

Afterword

It's unsurprising that my mother, by her example, was the strongest religious influence in my life.[74]

The Catholic college I attended had mandatory Thursday morning Mass. Dormitory fire-alarm bells awoke us; half an hour after being assaulted by fire alarms, most of us grudgingly trudged to chapel. Little more than thirty minutes later, we responded to the Priest's chant of "Ete Missa est" (The Mass is ended) with a most sincere "Deo gratias" (Thanks be to God)! I highly doubt this weekly routine was conducive to developing our religiosity.

✦

After graduating from The Catholic University's Columbus School of Law, I was associated with a Wall Street law firm for two years before returning to my alma mater as a law faculty member. But I had already applied to Yale Law School's graduate LL.M. program, so after only two years on the faculty of Catholic University, I took leave to spend academic year 1967–68 in New Haven, Connecticut.

Days before departing Washington, however, I learned that my mother had suffered a serious heart attack. That night, I drove to my parents' home on Staten Island. My father, Alfred Augustine Brown, was already in a nursing home, and my mother was now hospitalized, so the house was deserted. During my second day there, Dad also became hospitalized—though in a different facility. Summer was marked by daily drives between hospitals until early in August, when they were both discharged. Dad returned to a nursing home, and my mother went back home. Dad soon died, a victim of pneumonia as the final complication following many years of suffering from progressive Parkinson's Disease. The hardest-working man I've ever known, he was a fiduciary accountant for fifty years with the same downtown Manhattan law firm where his wife-to-be, Regina D. Welsh, was practicing law, as the first woman member of the bar from Richmond County/Staten Island, New York. My mother's doctor forbid her from attending Dad's funeral for fear it might kill her. My first

---

74   See "Catholic Parents Key in Transmitting Faith to Children," CARA, vol. 21, no. 2 (Fall 2015); and "Religious Development Begins at Home," CARA, vol. 9, no. 2 (Fall 2003).

Sunday in New Haven, the day before Yale Law School's classes began, came a scant month later.

After earning my graduate law degree, I spent the following summer collaborating on a writing project with a Yale faculty member before moving to Pittsburgh to teach. (Since Catholic University decided not to renew Vernon X. Miller for another two-year term as its Law School Dean, I had opted not to go back.)

My mother moved to Pittsburgh in 1972 and lived within a mile of me until a second heart attack claimed her life in 1977. During those five years, we related to each other more like old friends than as mother and son. She attended morning Mass daily at St. Paul Cathedral, and our paths would occasionally cross when I walked past the church en route to my office. No experience warmed my heart more than spying her at Sunday Mass and surprising her with a kiss when the priest invited congregants to offer each other a sign of peace after we had all prayed the Our Father.

Lesson One

Four decades have passed, and Eliza and I have been married nearly thirty-four years. Yet only recently did I note that my "falling away" began after my mother's death. Apparently this isn't unusual at such times of *spiritual desolation* when greater dependency on God must be acknowledged (which I failed to do).

Lesson Two

Perhaps because Eliza's family is Presbyterian, my Catholicism asserted itself after we became engaged: I insisted that the two of us attend Pre-Cana conferences together as well as regular meetings with a priest at Sacred Heart Church—despite my then being a "fallen-away" Catholic! These stubborn demands were selfish negotiations for *my religion* to be given equal weight and respect. Guard against this sort of behavior, especially if you're entering into a "mixed marriage." I'm glad we're married in the eyes of God and the Catholic Church, but feel fortunate that Eliza didn't tell me where to get off, given the way I comported myself!

Lesson Three

It surprises me that God has been so generous—beyond blessing me with a wonderful wife and three amazing children—by tirelessly showering me with grace despite my repeatedly refusing to accept. And now I get to revel in this astonishingly blissful period of exposure to what a prayerful existence can offer . . . *as can you!*

Do you like surprises?
You'll love God's surprises!
Eventually, I guess, we'll learn not to be surprised;
we'll realize that it's just God
. . . being God.

Acknowledgments

It bears repeating that much of this book was ghost-written. *Laus tibi, sancta spiritu* (Praise be to You, Holy Spirit)!

My wife Eliza Smith Brown, a Presbyterian who works with The Association of Theological Schools, encouraged me with her interest and curiosity about this book. I cannot thank her enough for making editorial suggestions, tirelessly typing draft after edited draft, and most importantly, always being the light at the end of my long, dark tunnel, patiently drawing me out (without ever, not even once, berating or embarrassing me!).

Our children were also instrumental. Will, whose moral fiber is impressive and admirable, especially helped with "Temptation." Brendan gave freely of wordsmithing skills and posed intellectual challenges to some tenets of my faith (provoking me to develop stronger foundations). Both sons questioned my materialism and expressed thoughts concerning the sometimes morality-blinding money-focus of capitalism—which served to improve my own values. Regina, whose dedication to purpose and determination to excel is always inspirational, sets the standard for us to emulate.

Father Joseph Freedy gave generously of his time as director of vocations for the Archdiocese of Pittsburgh, and it was he who first suggested that I write about my faith.

The priests of Sacred Heart Church delivered homilies that often hit home, for which I thank Father Robert Grecco (Pastor), Father Stephen Palsa, Father Ed Litaveck, Father David Rombold, Jr., Father James McCloskey, and Father Richard Terdine—as well as our deacon, John Vaskov (whose shining example led me to consider becoming a deacon). Thanks also to Father Thomas Gramc and Pastor Chris Stubna at St. Paul Cathedral in Pittsburgh. In the same vein, Rev. Edward Bryce, Pastor of St. Bede Church in nearby Point Breeze, Rev. John Foriska, Pastor of Holy Trinity Parish in Ligonier, PA (near *Trifol* retreat house), and Rev. Joseph Santos, Jr., Pastor of The Church of the Holy Name of Jesus in Providence, Rhode Island (near Brown University, where Regina studies) were likewise helpful. Collectively, many memorable sermons from these holy men were worth writing about. I hope my efforts have done them justice, and apologize for any failures in recalling or recounting their messages.

Sister Carole Riley, Executive Director of The West Virginia Institute for Spiritu-ality, provided endless encouragement and spiritual counsel week-by-week. Thanks to Dr. Carol E. Lytch, President of Lancaster Theological Seminary, for listening critically to my reading of the first draft of my Introduction, for providing me with much-needed positive reinforcement, and for introducing me to Dr. Riley!

Since a manuscript requires a publisher to become a book, I owe Dr. Sebastian Mahfood, OP, of En Route, my profound appreciation. He also favored me with the most thorough, thoughtful and insightful editing skills of Dr. Ronda Chervin, Emer-itus Professor of Philosophy, Holy Apostles College and Seminary. I feel extraordi-narily blessed to have had their cooperation on this project.

My heartfelt appreciation extends to all, together with all my love.

About the Author

William J. Brown, a multiple "excellence in teaching" awardee whose primary field of expertise is Federal tax law, graduated from The Catholic University of America, Columbus School of Law (J.D., 1963) and also served on its faculty (1965–1967). He earned an LL.M. from Yale Law School in 1968, then taught at the University of Pittsburgh School of Law for more than thirty years before becoming Professor Emeritus. Thereafter, he served as Director of the Graduate Taxation Program in Donahue Graduate School of Business at Duquesne University for six years. Professor Brown and his wife Eliza Smith Brown reside in Pittsburgh, Pennsylvania. They have two sons and a daughter, all in their twenties, and a Beagle-mix rescued dog named Knox. Bill enjoys running with friends as well as various artistic pursuits including pottery, charcoal drawing, painting, and restoring/refinishing/recycling old wood furniture.

Excerpt from the Weekly Bulletin of
Sacred Heart Church, Pittsburgh, PA:

Sacrament of Baptism

Pre-Baptismal program required for parents; sacrament celebrated on 2nd and 4th Sundays of the month (by appointment) at 1:00 p.m.

Sacrament of Matrimony

The Diocese requires a 6-month preparation period; a pre-marriage course is also required for each couple.

Parish Membership

Every family and adult should be registered as a practicing member of the parish. Please call the rectory for registration. Please note: you must be a member of the parish for 6 months before a sponsor certificate will be issued.

www.ingramcontent.com/pod-product-compliance
Lightning Source LLC
Chambersburg PA
CBHW022013090426
42741CB00007B/1016

9 781950 108633